UrBan Philosophy: Thought and Behavior System

Imhotep Fatiu

EVERYONE'S PLACE
1356 W. NORTH AVE
BALTIMORE MD 21217
410-728-0877

ISBN: 978-0-692-25329-8
ISBN 10: 0692253297

Gye Nyame Press

Dedication

I dedicate this book to my mother; the greatest mother in the world.

Acknowledgements

First, I want to acknowledge and give thanks to our Ancestors and give thanks for their on-going presence in my life. Secondly, I want to acknowledge the transformative power of African History and Culture. And thirdly, I want to acknowledge my wife (Ife Assata Fatiu), my children (Kawann, Antoin, Kwantese and Nyame), my Mother, my Father, my family and my comrades of the Pan-Afrikan Liberation Movement (PLM). Without these wonderful people, none of what I write within these pages would have been possible. Each person, in his or her unique way, has been conducive to the development and evolution of my thoughts. For that, I am eternally grateful. Thanks.

Table of Contents

Foreword

I met Imhotep Asis Fatiu at a mutual friend's house, in 2004. My friend and I were having a serious conversation about Bill Clinton being the first Black president. During the engagement with my friend, Imhotep was observing and listening off to the side (I could only imagine what he was thinking at that time, which he revealed several years later). After the discussion, he handed me a book written by Dr. Naim Akbar: Breaking the Chains of Psychological Slavery. He asked me to read it and to share my thoughts with him after I completed it. What he didn't know is I didn't have any intentions of reading this book because I was not on a quest for knowledge or self-discovery.

Ironically, I kept in contact with Imhotep over the years. I would see him at different places and he always had the same positive attitude from our first encounter. The year 2008 was a defining moment for me. I experienced a major crisis in my life. It was a reality check and it caused me to examine how I was living my life. Imhotep was the person I thought to call, because Bill Clinton was not going to come to my rescue.

When we talked I thought I was on the right path to correcting my crisis. He talked with me patiently and listened with care. That moment meant so much to me in regards to what I was feeling. He invited me to attend his study class. After attending study class, it didn't take long for me to realize that this visionary man was amazing; he was helping African people reconnect to their ancestral ways. I started attending his lectures and just like many other people, I was captivated and inspired by his clear understanding of the plight of African people, particularly in North America.

I regularly attended the study class, a sect of his organization P.L.M. (Pan- Afrikan Liberation Movement). During one of Brother Imhotep's study class sessions, I heard about P.L.M's organizational philosophy: UrBan Philosophy. I was captivated by it from this first utterance. I felt the connection; it sounded like something I experience every day. I just didn't know how to express it with such creative wisdom. "Life places you where you need to be, to learn what you need to learn". Hearing these insightful words put our entire meeting into historical context. Now I understood why we initially meet (back in 2004).

UrBan Philosophy inspired me. I began to diligently study African culture to learn about our indigenous ways. As a result of this, I later joined the organization. Meeting Imhotep Fatiu has giving my life meaning and purpose, and UrBan Philosophy has enabled me to put my life into historical context. As my understanding of UrBan Philosophy deepened, I realized how much I was in agreement with the philosophy. The idea of breaking away from the definitions of others and redefining from the correct cultural perspective was both appealing and inspiring. UrBan Philosophy is more than a book; UrBan Philosophy is a way of life.

Anani Kulu Fatiu
July 22, 2014

Introduction

UrBan Philosophy is a total system designed to liberate the minds of African people. This philosophy analyzes and challenges conventional concepts and establishes working concepts conducive to the African community. UrBan Philosophy challenges African people to think outside of the box. When African people live within a society whose "culture" produces perverted and nefarious people, the critical thinkers amongst them must examine why. When a society promotes oppression and exploitation, those seeking righteousness must deconstruct that society's philosophy. When that society's culture does not cultivate African people, then it's time for those Africans to construct a philosophy that is conducive to their development.

The time has come to embrace a philosophy that emanates from Authentic African culture and has been adapted to apply to modern-day life. UrBan Philosophy is that philosophy. UrBan Philosophy reconnects African people to their source. This book is more than a good read; it is a way of life because culture is pervasive. Culture is alive within everything. This philosophy takes a holistic approach to aiding Africans in rediscovering the African way. Any other philosophy which does not pertain to African people's holistic way of being should be rejected.

Everything about UrBan Philosophy is audacious, self-determining and creative; all the way down to its unique spelling. This entire book presents you with innovative concepts such as the general understanding of UrBan Philosophy, the description of an UrBan Philosopher, the tri-laws of wisdom, and more. It redefines everything from a cultural standpoint for African people to liberate themselves from what UrBan Philosophy calls "Psycho Bondage" and strive for self-discipline and ultimately, self-mastery.

African people come from a culture that cultivated and refined the people. It fostered self-mastery. European culture functions as an opiate to the African psyche, which ultimately obstructs our ability to evolve to our higher nature. It prevents us from realizing the true essence of ourselves. We are captive to an alien culture. In short, we could never truly operate as our cultural DNA was designed for us to do because we are disconnected from it.

We speak, think, and behave as something other than ourselves. It's wonderful for one to broaden her/his horizons and educate him or herself to the various cultures. However, there's no need to adopt a foreign culture when your own culture is intended to nurture, develop, and guide you.

UrBan philosophy states, "culture is both a people's incubator and compass." The direction that the people will go becomes clear once the people understand where they once were and where they are now. This understanding is arrived at from studying one's self. A person devoid of their culture becomes weakened and can easily be lead to self-destruct. The self-destruction isn't always perceptible when that person has acquired money, fame, material possessions, degrees, etc.; but the self-destruction is real. Self-destruction is inevitable when you are not operating as yourself. When you are unsure of who you are and adopts the ways of a foreign culture, you are self-destructing.

We should be perpetuating our legacy and adding on to it for the survival of African people. Our fancy cars, our big bank accounts, our job titles, and multiple degrees don't mean anything if they're not for the continued existence of African people. We are destroying ourselves mentally, physically, and spiritually by attempting to achieve a foreign definition of success. When your degree does not prepare you to erect institutions for your people, to be self-determined, to perpetuate your culture, then you are committing an injustice to yourself and your people, which further facilitates our self-destruction.

We are currently in a state of self-destruction on all levels. Our only hope of survival is to reconnect to our culture so that we can emerge out of the self-destructive lifestyle. We must be revived. UrBan Philosophy is the breath of fresh air that African people need be resuscitated.

Living in a society that is not productive, we've become contaminated with the un-cultivating ways of Europeans. We have taken on European ways to our detriment, but to their advancement. Although it appears as if we're benefiting, we are actually working against ourselves. We are unknowingly taking away from our own advancement; thereby, advancing another cultural group. UrBan Philosophy informs us that this type of behavior is indicative of "New Age Domestic Colonialism." We are unwittingly working to maintain our oppression. Studying the African way of life will open our eyes and influence change.

We are so far disconnected from our culture that we can't afford the luxury of not studying ourselves. We have to get to know us because we are suffering from cultural amnesia. Studying ourselves will not just enlighten us to who we are, but heal, encourage, inspire and obligate us to add onto our legacy. UrBan Philosophy states that "there is a healing principle inherent in African culture. Culture develops and evolves us; it defines us and tells us who we are." Therefore, without African culture "human growth and development will be arrested and human performance incapacitated". (UrBan Philosophy)

UrBan Philosophy is for the Pan-Africans that are in the trenches fighting the good fight for African people. Embracing this philosophy is a rejection of European philosophies and definitions. It's speaking, thinking and behaving as our culture instructs us to. There is a direct contradiction for a Pan-African to use a European philosophy to analyze and address African people. UrBan Philosophy states that it is a "nonconformity, non-traditional and non-conventional" mode of thinking. Thus, this philosophy is for revolutionaries. It is for the daring brothers and sisters who do not mind being different.

Embracing UrBan Philosophy is demonstrating that you are beyond the stage of just knowing facts about your culture. This is not a book that sits on your bookshelf to express to your visitors that "it was a good read." Admiring this philosophy is a start. The next step is to take on the challenge of applying it to your life because ***it is a way of life***. UrBan Philosophy "is consistent with Ancient African Deep Thought, and is infused with a Pan-African orientation. By extension, UrBan Philosophy is Ancient African Deep Thought adapted to a new area of time." The culture of a society structures the thought of the people and ultimately influences the behavior of the people. Our only choice as African people is to rediscover our cultural way (in thought and practice). Enjoy the contents of this book and allow the information to transform you by becoming an UrBan Philosopher. Your behavior will speak volumes.

Ife Assata Fatiu
PLM member
Co-Owner of Watoto Development Center
Co-Founder of Urban Youth Initiative Project
Founder of Facebook group Wake Up & Rise Up Sistahs!

Section one
General understanding

Why is it called UrBan Philosophy:

It's called **U**rBan Philosophy because it is the sole product of an **U**rBan existence. UrBan Philosophy grew out of the experience of an oppressive and repressive situation. Therefore, its total philosophical orientation is un-conventional and non-traditional! This means it doesn't conform to European philosophical standards. Rather it is consistent with Ancient African Deep Thought, and infused with a Pan-African orientation. By extension, UrBan Philosophy is Ancient African Deep Thought adapted to a new area of time. It incorporates the mode of thinking and ways of reasoning of Ancient Africa (the emphasis is on ancient to indicate a time before the advent of Asian and European invasions). Therefore, its line of reasoning and conceptual framework runs counter to Eurasian thought and ideology; thus, contrary to Euro-Asian philosophy, concepts and ways of being. It's a statement of rational rejection and an act of wise rebellion against the conceptual reality of foreigners. It is a refusal to be incarcerated by the thoughts, ideas and concepts of others.

In addition, it's called UrBan Philosophy because it's a revolutionary act; a self-determining action, in that, it's an act of defining and conceptualizing for self, in the interest of self, from the perspective of self. In this context the self that I speak of is the African-self. Thus, UrBan Philosophy is about thinking and conceiving differently, which rightly translates into being different. This means behaving different and interfacing with reality differently, which involves the use of authentic African cultural norms. This is what renders it UrBan Philosophy: it's an African thought and behavior system. A different kind of philosophy, which is a new and improved kind of philosophy! Therefore, it is nothing like traditional philosophies. For these are incompatible with ancient African Deep Thought, the essence of UrBan Philosophy. The best of African thought, reasoning and conceptual formation permeates the total philosophical framework of UrBan Philosophy.

Lastly, it's called UrBan Philosophy because it's culturally specific. Therefore, it speaks to and for a specific cultural group of people: the Pan-African community. Everything is culture; therefore, everything is culturally impacted and culturally influenced. Thus, it's only right for African people to have a culturally specific philosophy, conceptualized and worked out for their socio-politico advancement, economic empowerment and emotional-psycho-spiritual enhancement. All other philosophies seek to achieve the same for their cultural group. The difference is these other philosophies don't state their intent out-rightly as does UrBan Philosophy.

These other philosophies are culturally specific; however, they are pushed under the guise of universalism and neutrality. When in reality there is no such thing as cultural neutrality. Everything is cultural. Nevertheless, it is due to the belief in the neutrality of culture that African people are taught European ways of thinking and behaving. This is absolutely inimical to the African personhood! African people, by nature, are created to think and behave like African people; therefore, anything seeking to interfere with or disrupt this divine process must be averted and/or discarded. Thus, UrBan Philosophy becomes the means through which this is achieved, thereby, rendering UrBan Philosophy a philosophical necessity for African people.

What is the purpose of UrBan Philosophy:

UrBan Philosophy is designed to enhance and refine the thought process of African people; to add a new dynamic to human thought and reasoning. It is a liberatory philosophy that seeks to foster liberation thinking, amongst African people, to facilitate liberation: African sovereignty. Many Africans are bound by what Dr. Asa Hilliard labeled "conceptual incarceration." They are locked and confined within Euro-Asian concepts, ideas, ideologies, systems, philosophies and institutions. None of which are truly suited for the African mind. This is not to imply African people cannot benefit from Euro-Asian concepts, ideologies, philosophies, systems and institutions because African people can. However, none of these were designed and developed for the benefit of African people, meaning, none were created to advance the interest of African people. Therefore, African people must break free of the mental chains, intellectual shackles and psychological straightjackets of foreigners; thereby, escaping from the system of "conceptual incarceration". This can only be done by transforming the existing thought process of African people, which UrBan Philosophy seeks to achieve.

UrBan Philosophy grounds African people within an African reality; thus, centering them within their own unique worldview. Through the process of Sankofa, UrBan Philosophy returns African people unto themselves. This returning process, in essence, is a personal renaissance. It's a rebirth of consciousness; therefore, a rebirth of beingness. For a person's state of beingness is a manifestation of that person's state of consciousness. Sankofa is a Historico-cultural endeavor consisting of four vital phases: **Historical Journey, Historical Recognition, Historical Retrieval and Historical Utilization.** The logic is simple: Historical Journey is the intellectual search for the best of African cultural norms, Historical Recognition is the mental capacity to recognize and appreciate the best of African cultural norms, Historical retrieval is the psychological retrieving and spiritual assimilation of the best of African cultural norms and Historical Utilization is practicing the best of African Cultural norms for the empowerment of the Pan-African community. Therefore, Sankofa must be understood as a therapeutic process executed through the exposure to, study of and internalization of African history and culture.

UrBan Philosophy is an African philosophy, conceptualized with African people in mind. As a philosophical system, it exist to contribute to enhancing the quality of African life by addressing and rectifying the social, political, economic, psychological and spiritual maladies plaguing the African community. This will be achieved by showering and bathing African people in authentic African history and culture.

For culture is the prime factor and great imperative! Only through the injection and ingestion of African culture can the cultivation of holistic health and wellness be realized. Thus, UrBan Philosophy posits the use of African cultural norms as the model of African behavior to cultivate social competence, spiritual awareness, psychological soundness, political astuteness, and economic empowerment. The redemption, restoration and reformation of the African personhood are dependent upon the ability of African people to embrace, assimilate and internalize African culture. African culture must be the prime directive regulating and directing African life. In short, African people must re-learn how to think and behave as Africans. All of which UrBan Philosophy is designed to achieve!

What is UrBan Philosophy

UrBan Philosophy is the science of concept analysis. As a philosophy, it concerns itself with the examination and construction of new concepts to add to the progression of human thought, social-emotional development, cultural awareness and psycho-spiritual cultivation. However, understanding our usage of the concept UrBan is essential to understanding UrBan Philosophy. We re-conceptualized the concept urban, which is the kernel of the philosophical content of UrBan Philosophy. Therefore, ignorance of our conceptualization of UrBan will only serve to obstruct ones efforts to cultivate an understanding of, and subsequently grasp UrBan Philosophy.

Re-conceptualizing UrBan necessarily required re-defining it. We hold that our new and improved conceptualization and definition of UrBan is more specific, broader and extensive. That is, our concept and definition differs, socio-politically and philosophically, from the conventional concept and definition. Which in the final analysis, is vague and indistinct e.g. *of, in, constituting or comprising a city or town.* This really says nothing in terms of specifics! Thus, we resolved to re-conceptualize and redefine **U**rBan, in relation to socio-politico specifics, to render it a definitive reference. This is only consistent with the Philosophy itself, redefining and re-conceptualizing is at the heart of **U**rBan Philosophy.

There is a radical difference between our conceptualization and definition, of the concept **U**rBan, and the European conceptualization and definition. Ours have more substance. Not only did we re-conceptualize and redefine the concept **U**rBan but we altered its spelling. With our conceptualization, **U**rBan is always spelt with a capital **"U"** and a capital **"B"**. This is to distinguish our concept of **U**rBan from the European concept. The reasoning behind this is as follow: if our conceptualization and definition of **U**rBan differs from the conventional conceptualization and definition, then there should be an identifiable or distinctive feature indicating the difference between the two; thus, the rationale behind the capital **"U"** and capital **"B"**.

In addition to distinguishing the difference between the two concepts, usage of the capital **"U"** and capital **"B"** is also an act of audacity. As an act of audacity, it is a display of courage to be innovative, and as an expression of self-determination, it is a representation of us asserting our right to conceptualize and define for ourselves. For **U**rBan Philosophy holds, ***The Human being is a self-determining being.*** This is the unique thing about the human being: it can determine what is to *Be*. The future isn't fixed, but determined! Thus, we shall determine the concept UrBan. Therefore, UrBan Philosophy is a daring act of exercising creative thinking. The European way of reasoning and thinking is not universal. In fact, European thinking and reasoning is harmful to African people. Their mindset is materialistic, segregative, literal and linear. This type of thought process is incompatible with the true nature of reality; which is spiritual, integrative, symbolic, circular and holistic.

UrBan, as we define it, is an industrial city base: a specific geo-political setting. Therefore, ghettoes, neo-plantations, projects, hoods, shantytowns, slums; the deplorable and adverse socio-economic conditions therein (poverty, ignorance, illiteracy, un-employment, homelessness, drug abuse, criminality); the mentalities, attitudes and behavior tendencies engendered there from; the unique styles, fashions and dialects developing and evolving (as distinct modes-of-expressions), and the dynamic force of Hip-Hop comprise and are bound up in our conceptualization of UrBan. Thus, UrBan Philosophy is an UrBan organizing philosophy, adopted from and adapted to the socio-politico-economic milieu of African people (in the diaspora).

Our concept of UrBan refers to African people: the disadvantaged, dis-enfranchised, dispossessed, disdained, and dis-placed. This is whom we are referring to when we speak of UrBan. Thus, UrBan, by nature, is rebellious and revolutionary! It's nonconformity, non-traditional and non-conventional. UrBan is innovative and creative. Most importantly, UrBan is original! Bound up in its originality is the cultural imprint of African people, which runs counter to the ideologies, systems and institutions of Euro-America. In fact, the entire attitude, behavior orientation and cultural expression (of **Ur**Ban) stand in contradistinction to the worldwide European thought process and behavior systems.

UrBan is a state of consciousness (a mindset) shaped and molded out of, yet as a proactive measure against, an oppressive existence, which necessarily follows its own socio-politico logic. Thus, as a philosophical concept, **Ur**Ban is a distinct, yet systematic way of reasoning, perceiving and relating to reality (both objective and subjective). Whereas philosophy, on the other hand, is a systematic way of *Being*. For us, philosophy is praxis. This means our concept of philosophy involves and concerns itself with the merging of theory and practice. Thus, it is an attitude of mind and a behavioral code. It is the practice of an ethically sound and spiritually in tune orientation of life predicated upon a unique mode of thinking, regulated by a prescribed order, and dictated by a style of reasoning that follows and adheres to a clearly defined set of laws that governs rational yet disciplined behavior.

Philosophy, in this context, is philosophy as behavior. However, not any kind of behavior but behavior infused with high morals and sound principles permeated through and through with African deep thought; therefore, African Deep Thought is at the core of UrBan Philosophy. African Deep Thought is abstract thought, which is a mode of reasoning that includes synthesis and symbolic thought. It is a process of explaining and integrating reality, which involves cultivating an in-depth understanding of the under-lying principles of reality. Thus, understanding and explicating the cosmological truths of nature and the metaphysical principles governing the universe. African Deep Thought is the cultivation of spirit. It's about the transmutation of mind; converting the material mind into spiritual mind.

Philosophy is reflection, conceptualizing, inquiry, thinking and doing. It is both speculative thought and practical application; the practice of weaving intuitive knowledge together with empirical knowledge, to engender holistic knowledge, which involves integrating mind, body and spirit into an operational system of innovative thought and refined conduct. Thus, philosophy, herein, is not only an endeavor to explain and make sense of socio-politico-economic, cultural and cosmic phenomena; to provide a rational explanation of reality. It's also an endeavor to be a competent practitioner of reality through the mastery of knowledge, wisdom and understanding. Thus, African Deep Thought enhances the total person; it evolves you and brings out of you your inherent divinity. Most importantly, it teaches you how to be divine

Our idea of philosophy is the practice of wisdom; the science of being wise. The emphasis here is on *being*, for the idea is to be wise. This involves consistently demonstrating wise behavior; thinking wise, speaking wise and behaving wise. The operative function is wise; which, herein, implies doing: the execution of right-knowledge! Thus, whenever right-knowledge is consistently practiced right-actions are the results. Practice is crucial because wisdom cannot be taught; it must be learned through experience. The mastery of self-knowledge must be a daily sought after objective; a personal endeavor that can never be neglected. To do so is to preclude the discovery of self-knowledge, which is indispensable to self-actualization!

The prime study is self. You must study self to know self, and through the knowing of self you can be self (your authentic self; what you are by nature). Self-knowledge is an action, not an acquisition. It is not a level you arrive at but a state of being you become! It is a behavior, the result of being in tune with self, regulated and dictated by an acute awareness and sound understanding of self. The logic is simple: the better one understands self, the better equipped one is to give full expression to self. Self-mastery is the goal. However, you cannot master what you do not understand and you cannot understand what you do not study. This is what renders self the prime study. Self-knowledge is a prerequisite for self-mastery.

UrBan Philosophy is a different type of philosophy, and although termed a philosophy, it is not philosophy in the usual sense of what is meant by philosophy. UrBan Philosophy is a set of laws governing a distinct mode-of-thought, regulating a particular behavior orientation. Thus, UrBan Philosophy starts from the premise: everything is fundamentally conceptual. Concepts are the building blocks of subjective and objective reality. Therefore, UrBan Philosophy is conceptual reasoning. This, by definition, is concept thinking. Concept thinking is the practice of thinking in terms of conceptual frameworks. This, necessarily, include observing, analyzing and evaluating socio-politico and emotional-psycho-spiritual reality from a conceptual perspective and subsequently conceptualizing anew.

Thus, **U**rBan Philosophy is a system of thought and analysis concerning itself with the formation, function and influence of concepts on socio-politico and emotional-psycho-spiritual reality.

UrBan Philosophy uses an historical analysis to examine, decipher and interpret political, economic and social phenomena, in relation to the present historical epoch, in the interest of African people. It is the scientific study of concepts: political, economic, social, philosophical, ideological and cultural constructs. Moreover, **U**rBan Philosophy concerns itself with cultivating, developing and implementing innovative, creative and progressive concepts, relative to the present historical epoch, standing in contradistinction to the norm, conducive to stimulating critical thinking. This is at the heart of **U**rBan Philosophy.

The entire Philosophy revolves around cultivating and developing creative and critical thinking by way of concept analysis: the process of utilizing concepts in comparison to concepts to analyze concepts. Conceptualizing is a kind of thinking involving contemplation, imagination and creativity. To conceptualize is to systematically construct and formulate things within your mind. This requires critical thinking and deep thought, which demands discipline and focus. These are essential to the process of conceptualizing.

By its very nature, **U**rBan Philosophy is economic, political, social, cultural and psycho-spiritual. To be otherwise would render it a worthless philosophy. Therefore, as an UrBan organizing philosophy, **U**rBan Philosophy seeks to explain the conceptual mechanisms at work within a given socio-politico-economic reality, and subsequently conceptualize a rational, yet, progressive approach to said reality. Thus, UrBan Philosophy is a conceptual outlook on life in relation to the universe, with the understanding that everything is conceptually connected. By extension, UrBan Philosophy is a conceptual worldview. It organizes thoughts, shapes perception and informs outlook; it cultivates clarity of vision. There is a power in concepts. Not necessarily their construction but most definitely in their usage. Concepts can be used to attack and weaken or to defend and build up! However, the most important point to remember about concepts is: concepts are culturally imprinted. They are not neutral. Every concept is informed by and reflects its own cultural reality. Therefore, African people must conceive and use African concepts to optimize their interface with reality (especially an anti-African reality).

Not only is UrBan Philosophy a thought and behavior system, but it's also a social movement. What is meant by movement is it's an organized initiative geared towards achieving a single objective: **Pan-African Empowerment**. However, before this can become a reality the hearts and minds of African people must be liberated. Freeing the thinking and feeling of African people from the confinement of European thinking and feeling is the ultimate challenge. The task is to bring African people unto themselves so they can think and feel as themselves; that is, think and feel as African people. The question might be asked: how do African people think and feel? They think and feel as their ancestors thought and felt, that is, they think in alignment with their own cultural orientation and feel in accord with their own cultural disposition. What they are and what they do are dictated by their culture.

Human society is ultimately a cultural matrix, out of which thoughts, feelings, perceptions and actions are born. Therefore, thoughts, feelings, perceptions and actions are culturally determined. Culture is the prime directive, and the great determinant in all human endeavors. This is why the 1st phase of Pan-African Empowerment is the re-ascension and promulgation of Authentic African Culture.

Oppression and all of its devastation; all of its destruction, chaos and dominance, all of its mayhem and exploitation, in the final analysis, is cultural. The logic is simple: oppression is a behavioral system of dominance influenced and dictated by a particular type of thinking. Thinking is a thought system originating in the mind, and the mind is shaped, fashioned and molded by culture. Therefore, oppression is a cultural phenomenon maintained and sustained by the cultural suppression of African people. When this point is clearly understood and thoroughly grasped, African people will be better equipped to achieve their liberation because if oppression is cultural then it's opposite (liberation) must be cultural as well. Thus, the liberation of African people is dependent upon the ability of African culture to re-ascend as a living functional reality within the lives African people; to re-emerge as the predominant system regulating their lives. Because oppression is a negation of African culture; it is the denial of African culture and the coercion of European cultural practices. Therefore, the study and practice of Authentic African culture must be the order of the day. There can be no compromise on this point.

As a movement, the primary thrust and ultimate push of UrBan Philosophy is Authentic African culture. All areas of human interaction and engagement are cultural. One can never escape the impact and influence of culture; everything is cultural. Through culture we are made and created into who and what we are, and ultimately into what we become. Likewise, through the negation of culture we are made and created into who and what we are, and ultimately into what we become. Often times who and what we become, through the negation of culture, is something other than who and what we are by nature. Culture facilitates and cultivates maximum human growth and development. However, human growth and development is thwarted and distorted when culture is suppressed! Therefore, African culture has to be the watchword of the day, because African culture is **THE** only means through which there can be an overhaul of African people.

Only through the study and practice of African culture can there be a renewal of the African mind, a readjustment of the African personality, a realignment of the African character and a mending of the African soul. There is a healing principle inherent in African culture. Culture develops and evolves us; it defines us and tells who we are. Not only does it tell us who we are, it tells how we are to be. Self-knowledge is impossible without authentic African cultural awareness.

African culture is the way for African people. This is the single message to propagate and promulgate. Not only must we propagate and promulgate this message singularly but we must also exemplify this message consistently. We must endeavor daily to be African culture. It should manifest within our in thoughts, words and deeds. However, this will not occur automatically. In order for us to think, talk and do African culture requires that we shower and bath in African culture. We must consume it, digest it and allow it to nurture our being. We must live African culture because African culture is a living reality and only life can produce life. Thus, African culture is indispensable to African wholeness and wellness! In fact, the very existence of African people is hinged upon an African cultural renaissance. Not in the sense of a revival or rebirth of African culture because African culture is alive and well, but more so, as a widespread practice amongst African people.

African culture must permeate every aspect of life within the lives of African people. The total behavior orientation and mental disposition of African people must be influenced by and centered within an authentic African cultural framework. African people must be guided by African culture; our actions must be culturally determined. It's crucial for African people to adhere to their own cultural reality. African culture possesses a therapeutic value conducive to cultivating social competence, emotional stability, psychological soundness and spiritual awareness. This is the primary reason why we must push it unrelentingly. We can never waver in this endeavor. We must remain steadfast in our efforts to impress upon the hearts and minds of African people the necessity of African culture. Not European culture, Islamic culture or Indian culture (as in India)! No other culture under the sun except African culture. Our template and model for human excellence must be derived from African culture; therefore, our standard of human perfection must be found within African culture.

We must look to and search within African culture for all that we need. There is no reason for African people to search outside of African culture to meet their social, political, economic, psychological and spiritual needs. All foreign religions must be discarded!

UrBan Philosophy is a cultural phenomenon. It's a cultural movement that posits African culture as the primary reference and resource from where African people should refer to and draw from to address all of their problems. Inherent within African culture is everything necessary to weave together meaningful solutions for the issues confronting African people.   Bound up in African culture are the answers to life's problems.   There can be no true healing and wellness, within the African community, without African culture. It is the single most potent system we have at our disposal.   Through it, all can be achieved and the best can be fulfilled. African culture is African reality; thus, in the absence of African culture is the absence of African reality. However, the negation of African reality is not the negation of reality! We must still operate within a reality. Unfortunately, that reality is not African reality. It's a foreign reality, which by definition is a foreign culture. In fact, foreign reality, by virtue of its existence, stands in contradistinction to African reality. Therefore, it will not maximize the social-emotional and psycho-spiritual development of African people or deepen and heighten the cultural awareness of African people.

African people will not achieve self-actualization through the practice of a foreign culture! We cannot and will not realize, fully, our innate Africanity without African culture. Who and what we are by nature will never come to fruition nursing from a foreign culture. We will never receive the proper social sustenance, psychological nutrients, spiritual nourishment, emotional proteins and educational minerals necessary to foster a holistically healthy African community. This is so because foreign cultures were not conceptualized nor designed to cultivate optimal psycho-social-emotional-spiritual wholeness for African people. Foreign cultures were created for the indigenous people of foreign societies. For example: European, Islamic (Middle Eastern) and Indian cultures were created for the wellbeing of European, Middle Eastern and Indian people. Thus, the longer African people march to the cultural beat of foreign cultures the further removed African people are from their own culture.

Culture provides and brings order to a people's society. Culture is the socio-politico-economic and psycho-emotional-spiritual blue-print enabling a people to construct, arrange and regulate their society. Culture dictates the dos and don'ts, states the how's and whys and determines where and where not to go. Culture develops and directs. It is both a people's incubator and compass. Every society has its own ways of behaving, interacting, engaging and expressing itself; each has its own code-of-ethic and value system. It has its own worldview, philosophy of life and unique cosmology. All of this is an outgrowth from culture, and reflects culture.

Culture is not a hodge-podge of human interaction and engagement; it is not something haphazardly woven together without intent and purpose. On the contrary, culture is always intentional and purposeful; it serves a people's interest and fulfills their needs. It provides for their survival. Within Culture are the socio-politico-economic concepts and philosophic-spiritual precepts necessary for the construction, maintenance and perpetuation of a people's unique way of living. Culture establishes the standards of a people's collective behavior; thus, culture is the great communal sculptor. Therefore, culture is distinctive in that it manufactures distinct cultural groups. Culture provides a people with the know-how to interface with reality from their unique perspective.

Normal and abnormal are social constructs; thus, cultural in essence. This is so because; sociality is the human expression of cultural phenomena. Culture finds expression through human behavior, and behavior is a product of socialization. People are socialized through institutions. Therefore, the institutionalization of culture socializes people. Institutions are the primary means through which cultural norms and values are instilled within and transmitted to people. Family, educational, spiritual/religious and community are the primary institutions through which and by which people are socialized. Primarily, within these institutions people are instructed in the ways of behaving most suitable for the society in which they are developing and evolving. People are socially engineered through and by culture! Whatever we become is largely due to our ongoing exposure to a specific culture (culture is the determining factor).

African culture is order and refinement; it's a system of structure. It is a disciplined and principled way of interacting with one another and simultaneously interfacing with reality. It provides guidelines, protocols and rules of human engagement. It establishes parameters, wherein to operate, and develops behavior boundaries to adhere to. In addition, African culture is prescriptive! Ingrained within it are the instructions for psycho-social and emotional-spiritual wholeness. Within culture are the remedies necessary to foster health and wellness; therefore, without culture, there can be no emotional maturity, social competence, psychological stability or spiritual awareness. There will only be the reverse: emotional immaturity, social incompetence, psychological instability and spiritual ignorance. Thus, human growth and development will be arrested and human performance incapacitated.

Culture is a people's collective behavior system. By extension, culture is a people's life-system. It is the most essential system to a people. All other systems (social, spiritual, educational, military, political, economic etc.) impacting the lives of a particular people rest upon and are influenced by culture. There is no productive living in the absence of a people's Life-system to guide, direct and instruct them in the ways best suitable to optimize their existence. A people's culture maximizes their human potential! Therefore, for African people to be devoid of their culture (their Life-system) is to be devoid of their essence; that is, to be lacking the most essential thing that would render them healthy and whole.

African Culture is the essential factor determining the survival of African people. It is their foundation. Through it they are adapted to and prepared to deal with the harsh realities of life. Their culture instructs them in the ways of behaving most suitable and appropriate for their environment, by providing them with the know-how and equipping them with the necessary tools to meet the challenge of survival. Culture is the vehicle and instrument that makes it possible for a people to persist and perpetuate their existence effectively. Therefore, the core areas of Human Growth and Development (physical, emotional, spiritual, psychological and social) are cultivated and facilitated through and by a people's culture.

African culture fulfills the following:

- Encourage and promote optimal heath (physical fitness/exercise).
- Ensure and nourish emotional stability.
- Cultivate and maximize spiritual awareness.
- Foster and nurture psychological soundness.
- Forge and model social competence.
- Establish moral codes and ethical standards.
- Develop national consciousness and politicize the mind.

When a people's culture has been interrupted and subsequently disrupted, when they have been culturally displaced, their intrapersonal human growth and development will be stunted. This will have an adverse effect upon interpersonal human growth and development. Socialization will be corrupted and perverted, resulting in a retarded form of human interaction and engagement. The natural process of bonding and interpersonal intimacy will be obstructed and handicapped, rendering them socially incapacitated, which in turn will severely interfere with and impede the process of unity, and wherever there isn't any unity there cannot be a successful thrust against oppression. This means culture is indispensable to liberation. African culture fulfills the following three functions:

1st Function:

- To provide African people with a specific social orientation of the world. It situates them within a unique socio-politico-economic system wherein they are instructed and directed in the ways of behaving towards one another. Culture teaches them how to operate in the best interest of their socio-politico-economic system and subsequently informs them how they are to interact with and relate to other cultural groups (primarily their enemies).

2nd Function:

- To provide African people with the means (education) to successfully navigate through human affairs, endeavors and interaction, by equipping them with the necessary skill-sets to increase their chances of survival (productive living). It cultivates their innate potential and natural talents to maximize their overall performance as human beings, belonging and obligated to a unique cultural group.

3rd Function:

- To provide African people with a unique psycho-emotional-spiritual disposition about and inclination towards life. It fosters specific thoughts, perceptions and feelings about life, self, The Divine and their relationship with or connection to The Divine. African culture provides the guidelines and establishes the processes to facilitate African people's quest for self-actualization; attunement with their core. Thus, giving full expression to their essence.

African culture posits complementarity as the underlying principle of and operative principle within the African universe, guided by an inherent moral imperative. Thus, high morals and sound principles are at the heart of African culture. The implicit emphasis here is on quality relationships (complementarity). African culture promotes quality relationships on three basic levels, that is, good relations between humans, with nature and with the Divine. It is of paramount importance to strive for and maintain good relations within these three spheres of existence. This is indispensable to a harmonic African existence, which is essential to a balanced African existence.

However, the absence of African culture or the practice of a foreign culture precludes a balanced African existence. It's the culture that makes possible the existence of harmony and balance within the African world; not wishful thinking, blind faith or foolish hope! Within the culture are the tools necessary to maximize human potential, because the culture provides the social guidelines, moral instructions and spiritual systems to cultivate optimal human growth and development. African culture makes it possible for African people to live in sync with the natural world (human, nature and cosmos) and prosper as human beings.

UrBan Philosophy is a cultural initiative fundamentally about: 1) re-conceptualizing and redefining, 2) analyzing and challenging conventional concepts, 3) instituting new concepts and working definitions (consistent with a specific set of subjective and objective conditions), 4) providing rational explanations of existing socio-politco-economic conditions, 5) cultivating understanding of psycho-spiritual phenomena, 6) devising working solutions to the many ills plaguing African people, and 7) cultivating a new way of thinking and behaving resting upon African Deep Thought. Thus, our very existence is dependent upon the resurgence and survival of African culture. There has to be an on-going and never ending push for the study and practice of African culture. For African Culture is the panacea!

Section two
"GOD"

Perspective and Clarity

"God" is an abstract concept. This concept connotes and denotes specific qualities, characteristics, abilities, potentials and capabilities. It speaks to an unlimited ability to perform with proficiency: the efficient execution of force and power. Thus, "God" is an expansive creative capacity to influence, impact, perpetuate and evolve creation. It is not a separate entity existing neither somewhere outside of the universe nor outside of us; we are one with creation as well as creator. For the Creator Created Creation by becoming the Creation Created!

The "God" concept is a logical attempt to define the undefinable; an attempt to conceptualize the ultimate cause of "BEINGNESS". An attempt to quantify the unquantifiable! You cannot encapsulate the causeless cause; the initial spark that ignited the process of creation. One way to conceive of it is a Divine Universal Intelligence—a perpetual evolutionary orderly creative process—pure consciousness that permeate and constitute the entire universe. It encompasses, underlay and pervade everything therein. Therefore, it's intricately intertwined into the very substance that the universe is composed of: the quintessence of existence. One all eternal infinite enigmatic source manifesting its existence within, and as, the many manifestations of existence!

Within the many manifestations of existence therein lies a Divine manifestation binding or rather connecting the many manifestations together: a manifold unity. Therefore; all manifestations of existence are an integral part of one another thereby completing the Divine Creative Process. That which most people refer to as God, I understand to be the essential fundamental principle that makes up existence. Furthermore, it constitutes what it is to exist. It isn't a separate reality; an entity unto itself. There is no existence without it and it dwells within existence yet it is more than existence. The only place African people have to look (for what most people refer to as god) is within themselves; however, they wouldn't be looking for a god (something distinct and separate from them). They would be attempting to tap into that vast reservoir of Divine potential that lie dormant within them to access the Divine Intelligence of which they are composed.

African people are an integral part of creation, one with creation, wherein the Divine Intelligence dwells. Therefore, the quickest and fastest route to access it is within them because they are one with it. It is a process through which they attempt to gain total consciousness of the pure consciousness (Divine Intelligence) that make up their existence; an attempt to plug into its outlet thereby gaining access to their Divine faculties: omnipotence, omnipresence and omniscience. The idea is to unlock and awaken their inherent divinity, to manifest divinity, to be divine. This is the destiny of African people.

Creation is a product of intelligence; therefore, intelligence is always the agency behind creation. This means that creation, of any kind, presupposes intelligence. A creation as magnificent and vast as the universe is the creation of an equally magnificent and vast intelligence. By extension, the splendor, wonder, beauty, order and precision within the universe can't be the product of chance or serendipity but rather a divine Intelligence; a perpetual evolutionary orderly creative process, existing in and as the creation itself; intelligence and creation existing simultaneously as one. The latter is the manifestation of the former. Thus, creation is the material expression of the creator.

Creation is in a state perpetual motion; it's inherently vibrant and rhythmic. It's not static but dynamic. The underlying reality of creation is a Divine Intelligence, which is not static but dynamic. Thus, creation is a continuous process; it's not an end. It is forever changing and evolving, being made and re-making itself; re-shaping, re-molding and re-fashioning itself. The nature of intelligence is to create and creation is pervaded throughout and permeated by a Divine Intelligence. Infinite and absolute! Thus, Divine Intelligence exist before, outside of and beyond space and time; limited to nor bound by either. Nevertheless, it constitutes them both.

Creation is yet isn't; it's always in a perpetual and universal state of becoming; expanding and advancing itself. It doesn't stand still nor is it a fixed state of reality. Its very nature is a becoming; constituting what it means to begin yet never beginning or ending. Divine Intelligence is self-generated, self-created and self-initiated. It is the causeless cause; giving existence to all of existence through and by its existence. It is pure consciousness in a perpetual state of becoming, manifesting in and as all that is perceptible and non-perceptible.

This renders Divine Intelligence, creation and the African man and woman one. They are composed of the same fundamental fabric of the universe: pure consciousness. Notwithstanding, there are differences of life within the universe. Each endowed with its own unique and distinct level of ability, differing in extent, scope and magnitude; yet composed of this same cosmic stuff. The fundamental nature of existence, as well as all existing things and/or phenomena therein, are the same. Sameness is the essence of all subjective and objective reality. The material manifestation, the physical exterior, cannot negate the consubstantial oneness.

UrBan Philosophy does not espouse or subscribe to a GOD concept as a distinct entity existing separate from African people. The idea of an external, all powerful, independent being residing somewhere outside of the universe is not congruent with UrBan Philosophic logic. For UrBan Philosophy does not support nor does it promote the idea of separateness; dichotomies are inconsistent with African Deep Thought. Therefore, the concept of a dichotomized universe does not comport with the African worldview; it's incompatible with the African mind. The African mind is a symbolic mind and synthesis is its mode of thought-process. It posits: the universe is an organic whole; a living cosmos of which African people are a unitary part.

Section three
Operational Components

The Brain

The Brain is UrBan Philosophy's method of study. It consists of five fundamental principles. These principles dictate and instruct the overall methodology, which is methodical and painstaking inquiry into the fundamental components of a subject. This methodology is both a mode-of-study and an attitude about learning. It is not something done part-time; it has to be done all the time. For it's a behavior; that is, study is a healthy habit. Therefore, it is incorporated into ones entire educational orientation and approach to life. The 36th **Law** of UrBan Philosophy states: study is the great imperative in life. Study must be a part of the process of living. We live to study and we study to live. Our studies should enhance our lives in some capacity. The process of study should not be an empty endeavor but more so a promising pursuit. It should feed our intellect, nourish our psychology, enrich our spirit, and nurture our emotions. Our studies should empower us. We should learn from our studies by paying close attention to what we study. Thereby, identifying and discerning the useful lessons to assimilate and practice.

We study to cultivate learning. This requires a great deal of study, reflection and application. For in the final analysis, our studies should inform us, which should ultimately contribute to a new form of us; meaning, our studies should help to re-form us into something new and improved. If our studies fail to achieve this they're useless; therefore, a misuse of time. Whatever is studied should be of personal benefit to your social-emotional, psycho-spiritual and intellectual growth and development so you can ultimately be a benefit to the African community. This means there cannot be any random and cursory studies. Your studies must be purposeful, selective and thorough, which demands discipline and diligence. A certain degree of commitment to productive development is required; therefore, we cannot be lazy in the mind or neglectful of our studies. If we are to reap maximum rewards from our studies our studies must be internally motivated and not externally motivated. We must possess an internal drive, a desire for self-improvement as oppose to an external push to acquire information. At the core, our studies must be about human growth and transformation.

Study is a necessity of life. Within the UrBan Philosophical system of thought and analysis, study is engaged on a regular basis. One must critically study and thoroughly examine everything; commencing with the study of the African experience (history and culture). The study of this experience must be thoroughly understood and applied in relation to time, circumstances and conditions, from cause to effect. This is best achieved by adhering to a simple process: keep your studies in proper context, which enables you to develop a proper perspective, which in turn allows you to arrive at an accurate interpretation. After having applied oneself to the study of the African experience (thoroughly) then study the lore of other cultural groups (in search of the truth). This search must concern itself only with uncovering and discovering that which logically and rationally corresponds to objective and metaphysical reality. That is, discovering information consistent with universal law, divine order and cosmic truths. Furthermore, this information should contribute to developing an understanding of the true nature things.

The crucial aspect of study is learning. We live to learn and we learn to live. This is the prime challenge within the process of study. However, the key to successfully dealing with this challenge is to possess a sincere desire to learn. If our thirst for learning is strong enough we will be able to endure and overcome this challenge, and subsequently, learn from the experience. Learning is not an automatic function but more so a self-willed process. It doesn't just happen, it's made to happen. The degree to what we learn is determined by the degree to which we study to learn. The logic is simple: the greater the studies the greater the results and the lesser the studies the lesser the results. Thus, we are the product of our own efforts or the lack thereof. Whatever we want out of life we have to conceptualize it, strategize and devise a plan-of-action to achieve it. We have to go after it! We have to seek it out; we have to pursue it! We have to be relentless and unwavering. This is how we have to be about learning, which can only come about through the process of study. Therefore, to shirk the responsibility of study is to deprive ourselves of an experience of learning.

UrBan Philosophy does not confine or limit the process of study to a particular subject matter; study is universal. The search for knowledge, wisdom, understanding and truth, must be a broad, extensive and incessant process, yet centered. The act of acquiring, filtering, and assimilating information must be African-centered. Thus, it must be handled and processed from an African perspective, because there is no such thing as neutral information. All information is essentially cultural. It has a cultural imprint; therefore, a cultural impact. Information does not develop in a vacuum, to the contrary, information develops within a cultural matrix. This is the most critical thing that must be understood whenever studying. We must be clear of the cultural implication of the subject matter studied. To be ignorant of this will subject us to an alien cultural invasion of our minds.

Study is what refines and enhances us. Study evolves us! However, not just idle static study. Study disconnected from practice is insufficient. That is, study devoid of social engagement; social interaction and discourse, is not conducive to human growth and development. In fact, it stifles human growth and development! The human being is a social being; therefore, human growth and development is fostered and facilitated within a social context. Provided the social context is healthy and nurturing. Human beings grow and evolve best within a socially nutritious environment wherein they can engage in meaningful discourse and productive interaction. This means our studies must translate into doing. Our studies have to be action oriented; they must carry over into and manifest within the social sphere.

Our behavior must be instructed and guided by our studies. Otherwise, our behavior will be misguided by our lack of study or poor choice of study. Practice, the act of making productive use of the lessons gleaned from our studies, is an integral aspect of study. Study is empty and of no significant consequence if it is not link to practice. For it is the only way to validate or in invalidate what has been studied. Practice is the logical extension and culmination of study. It verifies and reinforces study. It also sharpens and enhances our studies because it reveals to us the strengths and weaknesses of our studies. Practice teaches us what to reconsider, what to discard and what to retain to further develop. It is only through study and practice we learn to master our studies and perfect our behavior. However, Africa must be at the core of our studies; all that we study must be filtered through Africa.

Study is conducive to progress. There have never been any great human accomplishments, pushing humanity forward, without study. Likewise, there will never be any major human advances without study. More specifically, there will not be any socio-politico-economic empowerment for African people without serious study and disciplined practice. We cannot wish and hope betterment into existence. We have to will it into existence, which requires study and practice. Blind faith is insufficient for the task at hand! Furthermore, systematic study is what enables you to remain relevant and effective. Study enhances and evolves you! It qualifies you! Above all, study equips you to perform competently. Therefore, under no circumstances should African people neglect systematic study and discipline practice.

The active awareness of this is crucial to the practice of UrBan Philosophy. The following are the fundamental principles of the UrBan Philosophical mode-of-study:

1ˢᵗ Diligent research:

- Execute your studies meticulously and thoroughly in pursuit of the truth, applying great effort and extreme care in the practice of open-mindedness, in search of the fundamental principles of a subject matter. You must be relentless at delving beneath the surface into the core of a topic, which requires a certain degree of commitment to knowledge, understanding and truth. Checking and cross referencing references, which require a great deal of discipline and focus. You have to take your studies serious! In fact, you have to value studying.

2ⁿᵈ Reflective and critical thinking:

- Practice contemplative and concentrated-thought; engage in the act of meditative, introspective and evaluative-thinking. This involves reflecting, seriously, upon what you're studying and looking beyond the apparent in search of its dynamic principles, to derive an understanding therefrom. Doing so requires taken nothing at face value, however, exercising the ability to discern between the literal and the symbolic nature of a subject matter. That which is of value is the inherent principles and not the outward manifestation.

3ʳᵈ Keen observation:

- Practice penetrating scrutiny, which involves a heightened active awareness of social-emotional, politico-economic, psycho-spiritual and cultural phenomena. Doing so requires acute intellectual vision. You must demonstrate a clear sense of perceptivity and clarity! This demands attentiveness to and solid focus upon your object of concern (topic, situation, event, incident, Phenomena, subject matter etc.).

4th Analysis and inference:

- Practice dissecting subject matter thoroughly without injecting your personal feelings to obstruct the process (your feelings must be calmed with understanding). Methodically break subject matter down (examining it internally and externally) to derive an understanding of its implicit and explicit meaning, and to determine its relevancy, to formulate a working conclusion therefrom.

5th Syntheses:

- Practice brining things together, which requires contextualization. All subject matter, (your object of concern) must be contextualized and integrated. This demands integrative thinking and understanding that all things are related (nothing is truly isolated, because all things occur within a whole; thus, rendering all things apart of that whole. Therefore, making all things related). You must connect and relate all subject matter (social-emotional, politico-economic, psycho-spiritual and cultural phenomena) to a larger reality: the plight of Africa people.

Study demands consistency. The search for and application of truth must be a constant practice. We should never abandon nor abort the mission of: 1) studying factual and practical information; 2) studying cosmic truths; 3) assimilating and internalizing such information, and 4) applying this information in our life on a daily basis to enhance our existence as a people. Study is our only course of action to effect socio-politico-economic empowerment and psycho-spiritual cultivation. The African cultural renaissance will emerge only as a result of systematic study and disciplined practice. Our progress as a people is hinged on it! If we are to advance, as a people, we must study! To neglect this great imperative is to condemn ourselves to an existence of misery and death.

The Will

The guiding mechanism directing the practice of **UrBan Philosophy** is the Will. The Will consists of five fundamental instructs of UrBan Philosophical practice. The Will is both instructive and directive. These instructs are an integral part of UrBan Philosophy's system of thought and analysis, and it's conceptual line of reasoning. The Will is the drive and force behind UrBan Philosophy. Thus, the Will is the faculty of execution; it instructs and directs the UrBan Philosophical practice. The Will informs UrBan Philosophical beingness! This renders the Will indispensable to the practice of UrBan Philosophy. Therefore; the following instructs must be intact, in place, activated and practiced simultaneously (anything less isn't **U**rBan Philosophy).

1st Instruct:

- Study in-depth and thoroughly examine concepts (ideologies, philosophies, doctrines, systems, ideas etc.) to determine to what degree [whether positive or negative] they influence and or impact society. To execute this requires selective and purposeful study into the prevailing thought systems (historical and contemporaneous) to deepen and broaden your

understanding of the existing socio-politico-economic and overall cultural reality.

2nd Instruct:

- Demonstrate a love of truth (cosmic knowledge,
divine wisdom and universal law) and the practice of
disciplined behavior, in the pursuit of self-mastery,
and spiritual awakening. To fulfill this requires an
intense desire to understand and appreciate the
metaphysical principles of the universe; the operative forces of nature.

3rd Instruct:

- Practice strict adherence to a flexible application of
logic and reason (intellect) in conjunction with disciplined emotions. To achieve this state of performance requires cultivating the ability to blend and
utilize thought and feeling together in a harmony;
creating an internal process wherein thought and
feelings work together, neither is subordinate to the
other.

4th Instruct:

- Diligently search for a rational and functional explanation (consistent with time, circumstances and
conditions) of all forms of socio-politico, economic
and spiritual phenomena. To do this requires practicing a holistic application of reflective thinking,
introspection, comparative analysis and historical
synthesis to derive working definitions and explanations of NOW.

5th Instruct:

- Endeavor to exercise calmness and maintaining a state of mental equilibrium whenever confronted with any adverse situation or faced with opposition, difficulty, or pressure (of any kind). To operate at this level requires the cultivation of self-control, mental clarity, a great sense of focus and purpose.

The Character

The Character is the outward expression of UrBan Philosophy. The character is the impression manifest with the practice of UrBan Philosophy. In fact, the essence of the practice of UrBan Philosophy is its Character, which is what UrBan Philosophy actually is. The Character is the total representation of the Philosophy. It consists of four distinct features. These features serve as a signature mark of **U**rBan Philosophy; an identifier of its practice. In essence, they are attributes. They pervade the entire line of reasoning. They're an integral part of its system of thought and analysis. They are interconnected; therefore, indispensable to the correct practice of **U**rBan Philosophy.

1ˢᵗ Revolutionary:

- **U**rBan Philosophy opposes oppression and injustice of any kind. For its ideological orientation seeks to cultivate, enhance and refine the African existence. Therefore, UrBan Philosophy is an ongoing push for Pan-African Empowerment, brought about by improving upon the social-emotional, politico-economic, psycho-spiritual and cultural conditions within the African world, while simultaneously addressing the ills within society and sub-sequently advancing the moral and spiritual quality of life. It advocates the radical yet progressive transformation of African people to usher in the restoration, reformation and redemption of the world wide African community.

2ⁿᵈ Instructive:

- **U**rBan Philosophy stimulates, inspires and engen-ders a solution-oriented line of reasoning. It directs and informs; thus, it promotes conceptualizing and redefining reality from a rational yet African-centered perspective, consistent with universal law and divine order. It urges and compels proactive measures, and the execution and subsequent manifestation of innovative, inventive and creative potential. It dictates behavior and prescribes morals, principles and ethical standards (from an African-centered perspective). Thus, it instructs ways of being to promote the health, wellness and healing of African people.

3rd Investigative:

- **U**rban Philosophy's range or scope of investigation is all-inclusive. There is no limit to its investigative practices; all concepts, doctrines, philosophies, ideologies etc. are examined (to better understand their nature, origin and evolutionary development). Moreover, all forms of social-emotional, politico-economic, psycho-spiritual and cultural phenomena are thoroughly studied, from a conceptual framework of cause-to-effect (with consideration given to time, circumstances and conditions). This enables the development of practical explanations and the subsequent conceptualization of concrete solutions.

4th Evolutionary:

- **U**rBan Philosophy is not stationary or stagnant; nor is it suspended at a particular place or era in time. It's dynamic. It expands, perpetually develops and modifies itself. For it holds that no system of ideas is relevant and applicable to all space and time. Therefore, **U**rBan Philosophy is a flexible philosophy capable of being adjusted and adapted; to make it applicable to each successive moment in time. It follows a rational course of motion, transcending space and time, yet not confined to any particular point, state or stage of development. Essential to its existence is a perpetual state of evolution; UrBan Philosophy perfects itself in time with time. It's alive; therefore, it matures with time and evolves.

The Constitution
36-Laws
Of
UrBan philosophy

The executive authority of UrBan Philosophy is its Constitution. The Constitution consists of thirty-six Laws. Law exist to establish structure and order. This is the fundamental reasoning behind the body of laws conceptualized for **U**rban Philosophy. These **36 laws** constitute the conceptual framework set forth to govern and give order to the practice of **U**rban Philosophy. In the absence of law dis-order arises! Dis-order interferes with and disrupts structural operation; thereby, strangling growth and development.

The 36 laws of UrBan Philosophy are a set of guiding principles that regulate, guide and direct the practice. They prescribe the thinking and reasoning of UrBan Philosophy. The first three are its foundation and all subsequent laws are a logical outgrowth therefrom.

1st Law
Creation is a conceptual design

Creation, in all its various manifestations, is conceptual. Everything is, ultimately, a concept. Concepts are the building blocks of, both, objective and subjective reality. Thus, immaterial and material reality originated in the divine mind of Ptah. Everything commences in a conceptual state. Institutions, traditions, ideologies, philosophies, religions, rituals, morals, principles and even the social dynamic of culture are all conceptual constructs. Therefore, social reality is a conceptual construct. Everything that exist was conceived, thus, rendering everything conceptual.

2nd Law
Concepts determines perception

That which is perceived is the result of how it is conceived; conceptual reality dictates and determines perceptual reality. Therefore, if your concept of something is distorted then your perception thereof will be distorted likewise. Concepts wield a tremendous degree of influence over perception. Thus, in the final analysis, your concept of objective reality will determine how you perceive objective reality, and by extension, how you perceive objective reality will determine how you approach and deal with objective reality.

3rd Law
Power is a conceptual dynamic

The ability to conceptualize and give concrete expression to a concept is an act of power. It's an erroneous belief to think of power in terms of things or stuff (material possession). Power is about possessing the mental capacity to conceive, formulate and organize a set of concepts into a functional reality: to exercise thought in a calculated mode to effect a desired end, to realize a conceptual design, is an expression of power. In the final analysis, power is about conceptualizing and defining phenomena and giving validity to that which has been defined or conceptualized.

4th Law
Reality is interconnected

Reality is that which is; a state of immaterial and material be-ingness. The conceived and the perceived, the tangible and the intangible, are both reality. Everything is reality. Reality is a unity; therefore, reality is one. It is a connectedness.

Thus, the conceived and the perceived, the tangible and the intangible are fundamentally composed of the same stuff. Everything is the same in essence; thus, rendering everything the same. This, in turn, renders everything connected.

5th Law
Consciousness is motion

Information and knowledge does not constitute consciousness. They are useful in the development of consciousness but they are not what consciousness is. Consciousness is determined by the quality of our actions; therefore, in this sense, consciousness is understood as active awareness. It is the ability to conduct and regulate oneself in accordance with wise decisions. Consciousness informs you as to what you should or should not do, when or when you should do it and how and how not to do it; thus, consciousness is made manifest in actions. It's progressive and proactive awareness.

6th Law
Life is a multitude of lessons
constituting the lesson of life

The lesson of life lies in experience. To live is to learn. However, one learn best when he or she study his or her experiences, and by extension, the experiences of others. Each experience is a unique journey to be examined and analyzed, for therein lie the lesson. Life is the ultimate lesson in that it constantly presents one with numerous problems to be resolved (from which lessons are derived). Life is the prime study. Everything about it, if properly understood, is a learning experience. This renders life a lesson. Throughout the entire process of living, one learns (indirectly or directly). The events leading up to one's present situation, whether favorable or non-favorable, the path that brought one to his or her current state, whether productive or non-productive, was a journey filled through-and-through with lessons.

7th Law
Struggle is a fact of life

Nothing develops, advances, come into existence or maintain and sustain its existence, without going through a succession of struggle. Nothing is achieved or accomplished without struggle. Every aspect of life involves struggle; it's pervasive and inevitable. Struggle is natural. Growth and development involves positive struggle, and likewise the maintenance and sustenance of development involves struggle. Thus, struggle is an inescapable process. Struggle molds and shapes us into who and what we are. Struggle is inherent in life.

8th Law
We are our experiences

Whatever we are is largely due to whatever we've experienced and partly due to how we've responded and reacted to what we've experienced **(indirect or direct).** Whether the experience is political, social, economic, educational, emotional, spiritual or cultural, we are affected by it (in some shape, form or fashion). Each experience molds us. By extension, we are affected and impacted by the experiences of our ancestors also, these molds us as well. Thus, we are a manifestation of how we assimilate and apply the process of a continuum of direct and indirect experiences.

9th Law
Knowledge is everywhere and forever

Knowledge is forever present and always around us. Knowledge is infinite and cannot be circumscribed. Knowledge is simply a matter of knowing. Therefore, ones studies must be broad, extensive and universal. Knowledge can be discovered and acquired everywhere forever. The root word of knowledge is "know" and knowing is an infinite process. Limitations are self-imposed. One can know whatever he or she seeks to know (productive or non-productive). The potential for knowledge is all around and within us. Possessing the capacity to learn to know or possessing the ability to intuit to know is the challenge.

10th Law
Balance is the key to life

The universe is balance. Although composed and consisting of different elements, the universe is, nonetheless, a state of balance. Thus, humanity is faced with the great challenge of re-creating within a human context the balance manifest within, and of, the universe. Balance is harmony, and harmony fosters ease. Harmony is a state of order, which is the absence of chaos and confusion. Order allows for productive development and progress. Balance is evenness. Evenness is when every aspect of one's life blends, and works together (neither is conflicting with nor obstructing the other). Therefore, balance is a state of human existence wherein all of your affairs and endeavors are harmonized. Thus, in the final analysis, a balanced life is an ordered life, which cultivates a life of ease.

11th Law
The human being is a self-determining being

The future is now, and now is determined. Human beings determine the quality of human existence. The future isn't pre-determined; thus, the future is subject to the influence and will of human beings. Therefore, human beings are the ultimate controllers of their destiny. We determine what will be, productive or non-productive, by the decisions and choices we render. Thus, we determine the state of our own reality. We are endowed with the power to construct and create whatever we desire; we can will into existence whatever we can conceive. We are the architects and engineers of our existence.

12th Law
History is perpetual

History proceeds un-interrupted. History is forever present, constantly made and always occurring. It isn't some isolated point in time, separate and detached from the present and the future. On the contrary, history is connected to and is an integral part of them both. History is the past, present and future existing simultaneously at the same time: **now.** Thus, history as a continuum is forever and forever is now. Now is always and always is eternal; therefore, eternal is now. This, in the final analysis, renders history always, forever and eternal. Therefore, history is a perpetual occurrence. History doesn't stop!

13th Law
Death is life

Death is inevitable. It is inextricably tied to the cycle of life. Death is not the cease of existence but rather the beginning of a new existence. The end is always a beginning. Life is a part of the Creator; therefore, life is always. Death is bound up within the process of life as transition and transcendence. Death does not constitute the end of life. On the contrary, death is a higher, more refined, form of life (not perceptible to the physical eye). Life and death are two aspects of existence. Life is perpetual; therefore, death isn't an ending.

14th Law
Everything has purpose

If it exists, it serves purpose. The moment something comes into existence it has purpose. The favorable and non-favorable, the productive and non-productive, all serve purpose at its initial point of existence. Thus, everything within existence serves purpose for someone or something. Purpose is inherent in existence. Existence is purpose. Therefore, existence, of any kind, is purposeful. Purpose is all around us, and we're purposed filled. Thus, our challenge is to discover a productive purpose and serve it well.

15th Law
Life is fundamentally simple

Due to ignorance, misconceptions and distorted notions about life, the simplicity therein is complicated. Life is a relatively simple process replete with challenges. These challenges are a necessary part of life and essential to one's growth and development. Life is an ordered and well regulated process constructed to operate smoothly; thus, the less one understands about life the more complicated life appears to be. The process of life is such that it proceeds orderly according to its law of governance. Thus, to understand the process of life is to simplify your life. The simpler your life the easier it is to navigate through life.

16th Law
Life is a paradox

Ignorance distorts and disrupts ones interface with life; therefore, what seems be is not always what it seems to be. Thus, just because a situation is non-favorable does not mean it's not beneficial. Benefits can be reaped from non-favorable situations; it's a matter of how one process and responds to the situation. However, this works in the reverse as well: all favorable situations are not necessarily beneficial. This is also a matter of how one process and responds to the situation. Therefore, life is rarely what it seems to be. Often times what is isn't and what isn't is.

17th Law
Non-existence is non-existent

Non-existence, in the absolute sense, is non-existent. There is always existence in the form of existence. Stuff and things, the tangible, do not define the totality of existence. Existence defines itself. Everything changes and undergoes conversion and transformation. Nothing stays the same. No thing, in the absolute sense, ceases to exist. There are always remnants and vestiges attesting to the previous existence of something or someone. Things move from one stage, phase, level or state of existence infinitely, transcending and transitioning into other stages, phases, levels or states of existence. There is no such thing as non-existence (in the absolute sense).

18th Law
Perception determines response

However you perceive a situation will determine how you respond to that situation; therefore, your perception of life determines how you respond to life. Your response to something or someone is always dictated by your perception. Thus, if you perceive it to be danger then you will respond to it as danger. Likewise, if you perceive it to be harmless then you will respond to it as harmless. Perception is inextricably tied to response; you respond to something according to how you perceive it to be. Thus, perception affects behavior.

19th Law
Everything is and isn't

Life is not always what it seems. Nor is appearance always reality. In some instances up is down and down is up (depending upon the position of the viewer). Therefore, in essence, they are the same phenomenon. Something that appears bad can have a beneficial outcome and something that appears good can have an adverse effect. Everything is and isn't! A non-favorable situation can have a favorable outcome (if processed correctly). On the other hand, a favorable situation can prove to be non-favorable (if processed incorrectly). There are times when favorable can be non-favorable and non-favorable can be favorable. Even to the degree that what seems to be progress can be regress, and regress can be progress. Thus, everything is what it is and at the same time everything is not what it is; nothing is absolute.

20th Law
Everything is relevant

Everything has relevancy. Just because it's not relevant to you doesn't mean it's not relevant to someone else. Thus, everything is relevant to someone and for something. The good, the bad, the favorable and the non-favorable are all relevant to someone and for something. Relevancy is subjective, yet a reality. Therefore, understanding the relevancy of things, even when not relevant to us, enables us to understand things. Nothing is without relevance.

21st Law
Everything Teach

Everything teaches something (whether beneficial or non-beneficial) we can learn something from everything. Thus, everything is teacher at some point and to some degree. The vicissitudes of life teaches. To live is to be presented with an opportunity to be taught by life. Circumstances, situations and conditions teach! Experiences teach! Life is replete with teaching moments. Some things are taught directly and other things are taught indirectly. Therefore, it is of paramount importance to pay close attention to life; to be extremely attentive, observant and vigilant at all times. Nothing in life should be taken for granted, for all therein teach. Both, favorable and non-favorable situations teach! Losses and gains teach. And equally so, the idiot, fool and imbecile teach. All under the sun teach but is not necessarily conscious of it. Thus, every teaching moment is not the result of conscious initiative; some are the result of circumstances and conditions.

22nd Law
The universe is order

Universal order is the way of the universe; therefore, everything about the universe is order. There is an inherent stillness within and of the universe; thus, a natural balance. The universe is a state of harmonic stability; thus, the natural order of the universe is stable. Therefore, everything within and of the universe operates in accord with a stable order. Even the supposedly chaotic states of reality are governed by a subtle operative order. Nothing is truly chaotic (in the absolute sense). All states and aspects of reality are governed by and follow a universal order. Order underlies, permeates, pervades and governs the natural universe.

23rd Law
Thinking is an art

Thinking is a learnt process; it is an acquired skill. It is a particular mental faculty that you must learn to use. You are not born a thinker; you are only born with the potential to think. Thinking is not an automatic reflex. It doesn't develop naturally; thinking is fostered. Thus, functioning according to habitual behavioral processes does not constitute thinking. Thinking is deliberate thought, which includes will and intent. On the other hand, functioning is conditioned responses, which is devoid of will and intent. Functioning is unconscious whereas thinking is conscious; therefore, functioning is bondage and thinking is freedom. Thinking is a cultivated ability. Therefore, thinking involves deliberation, critical thinking, evaluative thought, analytical application, assessing, conceptualizing, symbolic process-ing and synthesis. Ultimately, thinking is praxis; thus, think-ing is behavioral.

24th Law
Actions are self-defining

All actions tell a story; they communicate a message. Actions are self-explanatory, in that, they are the message they covey. For instance, negative actions are negative. All that is re-quired to establish this fact is to observe the actions. Actions don't lie! In fact, actions are truthful. They are whatever they manifest as. If the actions are positive you will know that by the positive impact of the actions. Even manipulative and deceptive actions are truthful actions, in that; they always re-veal their manipulative and deceptive nature at some point. Thus, the nature of the action validates the action. However, the impact of the action defines the action, which renders ac-tions self-defining.

25th Law
Life is logical

Life adheres to its own process; it has its own order of op-eration. It follows its own logical sequence. Everything within life flows according to its own rhythm. Life is pro-cessional and is replete with a series of challenges. Life is a simple process complicated by ignorance. The less we know and understand about life obstructs our execu-tion thereof. Living becomes problematic when we do not understand the process of life. Life is as easy as we un-derstand it and as complicated as we do not understand it.

Everything about life follows a unique order to ensure the order of life. The better we understand this order is the better we will understand life. Life didn't just happen randomly without purpose. On the contrary, life is a purposed filled phenomenon. Life is a divine challenge designed to cultivate the best within human beings. Life presents us with natural problems to solve to enhance our intelligence. None of which is haphazard; thus, through the process of life human growth and development is fostered in accord with the logical flow of life. When life is properly understood, all outcomes are logical outcomes.

26th Law
Creation is perfection

Creation is perfect, in that, its overall cosmic design is flawless. The great grand scheme of existence is perfectly woven together. Creation is masterfully engineered and crafted; everything is exactly the way it should be, and where it should be to ensure a fluent universal flow of energy. Thus, the natural flow and universal order of the universe is perfect. This means the divine laws that oversee, regulate and govern all things are perfect. Perfect is the universe! The cosmic essence underlying reality is perfect. There is nothing wrong with or out of place within creation. Everything has its place and serves its function within creation. Not man made creations (circumstances, situations and conditions), but natural creation; the cosmic design of real reality! The divine architectural structure of creation is perfect. There aren't any glitches, flaws or imperfections within creation. It's skillfully sculptured and its movements are expertly choreographed.

27th Law
Nature is balance

Nature is balance, governed only by its laws to ensure a state of stability. Therefore, the natural is in a perpetual state of equilibrium; everything is working together to maintain and sustain a state of universal stability. Thus, nature is stable! All natural phenomena, cosmic processes and/or forces of nature exist in accord with the natural design of creation. Phenomena are in order, processes are in alignment and forces of nature are synergistic. Everything in and of nature is naturally stable; everything is balanced! Balance is the way of nature when left alone! Everything occurring within nature occurs in accord with a natural state of balance to maintain and sustain universal balance. This means imbalance is unnatural; therefore, not of nature!

28th Law
The human being is a divine being

The human being is a unitary part of the *Divine*; thereby, rendering the human being a divine being. As a unitary part of the *Divine*, the human being is endowed with the ability to do as the divine, not necessarily on the same scale or to the same degree. However, the human being can manifest masterful creations and the human being's ability to know is endless. The human being's capacity for learning is unlimited, the human being's imagination is boundless and the human being's mind is infinite. The evolutionary capacity of the human being is forever. This means the human being can evolve forever; the human being can forever outstrip itself. Therefore, the human potential for growth and development is un-restricted, meaning, the human being can constantly grow and develop within its divinity. At the core of the human being therein lies the *Divine*. Thus, human divinity is predicated upon the oneness between the Divine and the human being.

29th Law
Harmony is natural

The universe exists in a state of harmony; therefore, harmony is the natural state of the universe. Creation is harmonized! The cosmos is a state of harmony. Harmony exists throughout the universe; thus, harmony is inherent within creation. Harmony is a Divine state of existence that came into existence at the beginning of existence. Thus, harmony is the initial state of being! In fact, harmony sustains creation and orders the universe. This means the universe operates harmoniously on the basis of order. All of the processes and phenomena, therein, work in harmony. The universe is harmony!

30th Law
Belief dictates behavior

Belief can either motivate you or stagnate you. Whatever you believe will determine what you will do. We act according to our convicted beliefs (not professed beliefs). If you believe you can achieve and succeed you will achieve and succeed. And if you don't believe you can achieve and succeed you won't achieve and succeed. You are only as great as you truly believe you are! Belief is more than a mental act, belief is an actual act. Belief wields a great deal of influence over behavior. In fact, belief and behavior are inter-locked. The consequence of behavior is often times the result of belief.

31st Law
Communication is Supreme

Communication gives life meaning. Communication is the great conveyor of thoughts, ideals and concepts. Communication is the social means through which human interaction is mediated; therefore, communication makes human interaction possible. Communication is a necessity of human existence, it facilitates social intercourse. Thus, communication is essential to progress; there can be no great advancements in human society without communication. Creation is the product of communication. Not just any kind of communication but productive communication; meaningful and purposeful communication. Communication wields a certain degree of power: words have the potential to build and destroy. Words can either facilitate human development or obstruct it! Words are powerful. Communication is supreme.

32nd Law
Imagination is freedom

The imaginative mind is the free mind. Imagination is without limits; therefore, imagination is boundless. Imagination is not confined to any particular doctrine or ideology. Imagination is free of all forms of intellectual restraints and constraints. Nor is imagination confined to the space-time continuum. It's not locked within the here-and-now! Imagination is multidimensional. Imagination is expansive and malleable. It can't be restricted to a single form but it can conform to whatever form to retain it's free ability to be. If you can imagine it you can experience it. Imagination enables you to live on your own terms, not locked into a single reality, yet you can create and experience whatever reality you can imagine (but only if your imagination is healthy). A healthy imagination is a culturally sound imagination.

33rd Law
Life is a process

Nothing occurs immediately or happens instantly; nothing just appears in life. Everything in life develops, unfolds and takes place within the context of time. There is always a duration of time involved. Life is a process. It consists of a series of activities, events, situations, conditions and/or phenomena manifesting perpetually. Things are always moving from one degree to another, progressing from one level to another and evolving from one stage to another. Life is not static, it's dynamic and rhythmic. It has a cosmic flow; things happen and occur in accord with the universal order of things. The process of life is a cosmic process consisting of a multitude of processes.

34th Law
Obedience is a natural order

All natural phenomena, occurrences and celestial bodies within the universe are obedient to the universal laws of the universe; they function and operate in compliance with the natural order therein. They are all in sink; therefore, obedience is a natural universal function. It's inherent within the universe! In fact, obedience is the way of the universe. Everything within the universe is obedient to the systematic order of the universe; everything adheres to the cosmic protocol set in place within the universe. This means everything is naturally in order; thus, obedience permeates the entire universe.

35th Law
Mind is all

The entire material world is the manifestation of mind: the Great Universal mind. The human mind is a unitary part of the Great Universal Mind; therefore, mind is mind. Mind is the originator, initiator and executor of all human accomplishments. All things are made possible through and by mind. Mind achieves all! Mind is the supreme architect and master engineer of all creations. Everything is essentially mind. Mind is behind all things. Mind is the ultimate power source; therefore, mind is all powerful. Mind is the greatest weapon of all times! The causeless cause giving meaning to all things! Mind is that which enables you to BE! You are your mind. You can only go as far as your mind will take you; therefore, your greatest investment is in your mind. Therefore, a well cultivated and refined mind is supreme.

36th Law
Study is the great imperative of life

Self-mastery, unlocking or tapping into our Divine potential, is our ultimate objective. However, this is not a task achieved automatically. You don't just live and become self-mastered. Self-mastery requires a great deal of systematic study (both internal and external). However, study must be selective and purposeful. It must be engaged specifically to facilitate the process of self-mastery. Study is the only way we truly come to know ourselves and self-knowledge is crucial to the process of self-mastery. Without self-knowledge self-mastery is impossible! This is what renders study the great imperative, because it enables us to achieve self-mastery through the cultivation of self-knowledge. Therefore, study is an indispensable function to human growth and development.

The Wisdom
of
UrBan Philosophy

The Wisdom consists of 360 insights. These insights are Empowermental. They serve as enlightenment to enhance awareness and sharpen perception. Empowermental insights are designed to produce empowering thoughts to facilitate self-empowerment. They are not about spurring or inciting anyone to rash actions. They are not an appeal to emotions, although they do appeal to emotions. However, they are about empowering you by giving you your power back through facilitating the discovery of self-power. Self-power is inherent power, which is your innate creative capacity to create your own destiny. Empowermental is not in a dictionary, it is an UrBan Philosophical concept.

1st Insight: Information precedes knowledge; you must inform yourself in order to know. Knowing is a product of information.

2nd Insight: Do not be deceived by the appearance of something; appearance isn't necessarily what it appears to be.

3rd Insight: Potentiality is everywhere. Everyone is endowed with potential, yet potential is without actualization. Potentiality is in a constant state of becoming to arrive at actuality. Thus, actuality is arrived at through a constant state of becoming.

4th Insight: You come into existence endowed with all the ingredients necessary to manifest greatness. You are endowed with great potential to be cultivated for greatness.

5th Insight: To never attempt to do is to never know what you can do; thus, self-imposed limitations are a matter of never attempting to do anything.

6th Insight: Do not fear self-challenge but rather delight in the activity of challenging yourself. You are your most formidable opponent.

7th Insight: Live for today, yet prepare for tomorrow. Tomorrow is possible.

8th Insight: All things are possible, although all things are not probable.

9th Insight: Study the fool; the fool is a teacher too. He or she often teaches without knowing it.

10th Insight: Your *"Will"* is free only in the sense that it is free to be either under your control or the control of another.

11th Insight: All things depend upon one another; nothing is absolutely independent but more so interdependent.

12th Insight: Change is always a challenge. Therefore, to accept the challenge is to accept change.

13th Insight: Living is learning if you study the experiences you experience.

14th Insight: What you know is validated by what you do. Knowing is doing; therefore, to know is to do.

15th Insight: Self-affirmation needs no support or reinforcement.

16th Insight: Procrastination is a destroyer of progress.

17th Insight: Only an organized mind can produce organization; therefore, in the absence of an organized mind, there can be no organization. Thus, organization begets organization.

18th Insight: You cannot instill or cultivate within someone else what you lack and is devoid of yourself.

19th Insight: Always provide an authentic representation of yourself to the world; originality validates you best.

20th Insight: Contention is bound up in the process of life; therefore, to live is to contend.

21st Insight: Nothing is without meaning. Meaning just has to be uncovered and discovered.

22nd Insight: You are only as great as you think you are; greatness commences in your mind.

23rd Insight: You are that which is unique within the universe.

24th Insight: Everything can be improved upon; improvement is always possible.

25th Insight: Actions are self-defining; whatever you do or do not do defines itself.

26th **Insight:** Whatever can be studied can be mastered.

27th **Insight:** Progress dictates sacrifice; therefore, always be prepared to sacrifice to make progress.

28th **Insight:** The ultimate study is self.

29th **Insight:** Wherever you are, at any moment in time, is where you need to be to learn whatever lesson you need to learn.

30th **Insight:** Change your life by changing things within your life.

31st **Insight:** Complaining is a misuse of time. It offers neither relief nor resolution. It only compounds a problem by adding frustration to it.

32nd **Insight:** You cannot change what has occurred; you can only learn from it.
33rd **Insight:** You are as you perceive yourself to be.

34th **Insight:** Self-validation is the best validation.

35th **Insight:** You are your own standard of beauty.

36th **Insight:** Life is a series of consequences set in motion by your decisions; therefore, be careful when making a decision.

37th **Insight:** Life challenges you to be your best by challenging you to challenge yourself.

38th Insight: It is not enough to think positive. You must think positive and act positively.

39th Insight: You weave the web of your reality with your own thoughts.

40th Insight: You are the solution to all of your problems.

41st Insight: Whatever you do not bring under control gets out of control.

42nd Insight: Think not that you cannot achieve. You can achieve whatever you desire intensely enough.

43rd Insight: Information demands investigation. Through the process of investigation the accuracy and authenticity of information is determined.

44th Insight: You are what you do, and you become what you continue to do.

45th Insight: The greatest lesson of life is life; thus, the beauty of life lies in the lessons learnt therefrom.

46th Insight: If it's not developing, advancing or evolving, it's stagnant. Thus, degenerating, deteriorating or dying.

47th Insight: Your destination in life isn't as important as your journey. It is the latter of the two that enlightens you.

48th Insight: Every circumstance, favorable or not, is a learning experience.

49ᵗʰ Insight: Reality defines itself; therefore, the best criterion to assess reality is reality.

50ᵗʰ Insight: The essence of love is understanding. Its character is creativity and its personality is imagination.

51ˢᵗ Insight: Living is serious business; therefore, live your life according to a serious plan.

52ⁿᵈ Insight: Do not devalue your time through its misuse; therefore, expend your time wisely.

53ʳᵈ Insight: Whatever you get out of life is determined by whatever you put into life; therefore, if you do not put anything meaningful into life you will not get anything meaningful out of life.

54ᵗʰ Insight: If you do not know anything, you will not be anything.

55ᵗʰ Insight: Ignorance is a weakness that must be strengthened by transforming it into knowledge.

56ᵗʰ Insight: Disorganization is a manifestation of a disorganized mind. Thus, disorganization is the offspring of disorganization.

57ᵗʰ Insight: You are in and of the universe; therefore, you are one with it.

58ᵗʰ Insight: Victory is a state of mind. You must conceive and believe in your status of victory.

59th Insight: Life will show you what you need to see when you need to see it, your task is to see it and respond appropriately.

60th Insight: Self-doubt is paralyzing. It is a mental dis-ease that erodes self-initiative.

61st Insight: Pessimism is a contagious dis-ease that destroys hope.

62nd Insight: Mistakes are inescapable; however, mistakes can be minimized.

63rd Insight: Your word and your character are inextricably bound; whatever you say reflects and represents who you are.

64th Insight: Mental images become reality; therefore, make sure you control the images you entertain.

65th Insight: The notions you harbor within your mind manifest within your world.

66th Insight: The universe return unto you whatever you give unto it.

67th Insight: Interacting with the objective world influences thinking; therefore, be careful as to who and what you interact with.

68th Insight: Observation facilitates understanding; it's an art conducive to growth and development.

69th Insight: Never feel compelled to prove your worth. Remain true to yourself and your worth will be appreciated.

70th Insight: Always aspire to leave an impressive yet productive impact upon the world.

71st Insight: Always think of how you can change the world, and then set out to do it.

72nd Insight: Hear all but heed only knowledge.

73rd Insight: The beauty of memory is the ability to retain experience.

74th Insight: Love is an abstract concept that can only be known through actions.

75th Insight: The greatest service rendered is to serve the natural interest of your people.

76th Insight: Breaking your word damages your character.

77th Insight: Character is important and a good name is honored. They complement one another; therefore, always strive to preserve the quality of them both.

78th Insight: Be mindful of your thoughts; like minds attract and gravitate towards one another.

79th Insight: No one knows all things. However, all things can be known. Study uncovers and discovers all things.

80th Insight: Knowledge is the guiding principle; therefore, you can only go as far as your knowledge will take you.

81st Insight: You're a sum total of your thoughts; therefore, make learning apart of your daily activities.

82nd Insight: Knowledge is akin to light and light is that which enables you to see; therefore, get knowledge.

83rd Insight: Your environment provides you with invaluable information; therefore, forever observe your environment.

84th Insight: Life bestows its rewards according to your level of knowledge; therefore, forever increase your knowledge.

85th Insight: Never become content with your present level of knowledge; dare to acquire more.

86th Insight: Learning is a virtue that affords great rewards to the learner.

87th Insight: The acquisition of information is one thing, while the application is another. Thus, acquisition doesn't guarantee application. Application is an art; a learnt skill.

88th Insight: Communication is one of, if not, the greatest contributions to civilization. Therefore, always endeavor to use communication wisely.

89th Insight: It isn't necessary to accept all challenges; however, it is advisable to respond to all threats.

90th Insight: Actions are thoughts made manifest; therefore, actions change when there's a change of thoughts.

91st Insight: Ignorance places you at a disadvantage; therefore, seek to gain the advantage through the acquisition of knowledge.

92nd Insight: The cultivation, preservation and refinement of the mind is of paramount importance.

93rd Insight: True knowledge of self gives rise to power, confidence and authority.

94th Insight: Take nothing lightly. Remain vigilant, focused and determined at all times.

95th Insight: To try and not succeed is not, necessarily, failure. Failure is when you don't succeed and you stop trying.

96th Insight: Those who tame the mouth tame the entire self.

97th Insight: The parameter of one's awareness is determined by the scope of one's knowledge.

98th Insight: It is not possible to direct the course of another's life if you cannot direct the course of your life.

99th Insight: The serious man and woman are the immortalized man and woman.

100th Insight: Study all things. There's always a lesson to be learnt. Thus, even in leadership, remain a student.

101st Insight: The greatest of all investments is the investment in your mind. Thus, a well cultivated and refined mined turns great profits.

102nd Insight: Always do as you truly feel within, not as you think others would like you to.

103rd Insight: Research is healthy for the mind; never take anything at face value.

104th Insight: Whatever you set out to do be sure to finish it, never quit. Quitting is a degenerative disease destructive to your character.

105th Insight: To master self is to master the forces of the universe; therefore, seek self-mastery.

106th Insight: Never tell yourself you can't do something. With the guidance of time, hard work and practice you can learn to do whatever you desire.

107th Insight: Never follow a fool. For he or she can only lead you to destruction.

108th Insight: Never allow your mind to become stagnant; always place it in an atmosphere that fosters its growth.

109th Insight: To have another's perception of reality imposed on you restrict your ability to think and act independently.

110th Insight: Never be afraid to admit when you don't know, no one know everything. Not knowing is a natural phase within the process of mental development.

111ᵗʰ Insight: Truth is within everything; even within fiction and falsehood therein is an element of truth.

112ᵗʰ Insight: Carefully select your words according to the circumstance of the moment. There's a power in words; words can either build or destroy. The choice is yours however you choose to use your words.

113ᵗʰ Insight: Everything revolves, evolves or devolves; nothing remains in its original state.

114ᵗʰ Insight: Do not be afraid to ask questions. One of the best ways to verify the validity of something is to question it.

115ᵗʰ Insight: Reading is a process through which the mind is cultivated and developed.

116ᵗʰ Insight: Everything one is to know is already known yet undiscovered. You are a repository of knowledge.

117ᵗʰ Insight: Life does unto you as you do unto it; it is a reciprocal process.

118ᵗʰ Insight: If something can be learnt it can be taught; therefore, if it can be taught it can be learnt. Thus, if it can be learnt it can be mastered.

119ᵗʰ Insight: The mind can be conditioned and trained to operate at any capacity.

120ᵗʰ Insight: Seek the mastery of communication, it is the medium through which information is disseminated and ideas are exchanged.

121st Insight: All situations can be resolved. It's a matter of knowing how to approach the situation.

122nd Insight: The effectiveness of something is determined by its use, not its possession. The utilization validates its worth.

123rd Insight: Only the sincere of heart and understanding of mind can properly utilize information.

124th Insight: Determination aids those sincere about achieving their objective, not the insincere.

125th Insight: There can be no treachery without trust; however, everyone must trust someone. Therefore, the risk of trust must be engaged with great caution.

126th Insight: Whatever you want out of life, you must make happen; nothing just happens, there's a force behind all happenings.

127Th Insight: Life is a process determined by a succession of experiences perpetually unfolding.

128th Insight: Imagination is flexible and elastic. It has a boundless expansion capacity limited only by you.

129th Insight: You are the author of your story, written by the decisions rendered by you.

130th Insight: You are the tailor, seamstress and ultimate designer of your character.

131st Insight: You are treated as you allow yourself to be treated, and by extension, you allow yourself to be treated as you treat yourself. Therefore, learn to treat yourself divinely and you will not tolerate anything less than divine treatment.

132nd Insight: Understanding does not mean acceptance; therefore, always endeavor to cultivate understanding.

133rd Insight: Your life is a meaningful life. You just have to discover and uncover the meaning therein.

134th Insight: Be what you speak and speak what you are.

135th Insight: All concepts are not relevant or applicable to all space and time.

136th Insight: Growth must be nurtured and nourished by growth, to foster growth. Only growth can breed growth.

137th Insight: Always question; questions enable you to determine the relevancy and legitimacy of something.

138th Insight: Anger properly channeled is productive.

139th Insight: Reading is a necessity, it develops the mind.

140th Insight: Every action executed by you initiates a sequence of events.

141st Insight: Pride is a beneficial quality when utilized wisely. However, foolish pride can be self-destructive.

142nd Insight: Survival dictates: adapt, struggle and endure.

143rd Insight: The correct utilization of information is power.

144th Insight: Monitor your ideas. Premature ideas develop into mature idea.

145th Insight: If you do not know, do not pretend that you do; never speak out of ignorance.

146th Insight: You are endowed with the power to empower yourself.

147th Insight: Whatever you call yourself and whatever you respond to, speaks volumes about how you perceive yourself.

148th Insight: The world sees of you what you present to the world; therefore, be careful of your presentation.

149th Insight: Self-esteem and the lack thereof are expressed and reflected in all that you say, and do.

150th Insight: Self-perception dictates how you interact with and relate to others.

151st Insight: Thought initiates motion; therefore, your movement should be preceded by deliberate thought.

152nd Insight: Victory is a mental reality before it is an actual reality; it is a self-willed process commencing in your mind.

153rd Insight: The universe is meaningful; therefore, everything therein has meaning. Our task is to discover the meaning of all things to optimize our ability to operate within meaningful relations in relation to all things.

154th Insight: Despair not nor be dismayed, for you are a divine being. You are powerful!

155th Insight: Whatever the mind can't conceive it can't achieve. Success is conceptual, it's self-willed.

156th Insight: The joy of **BEING** is to **BE** because ultimately you can determine what to **BE,** for you are endowed with the ability to **BE** all that you aspire to **BE.**

157th Insight: You are responsible for you. Therefore, in the final analysis, you are ultimately responsible for your success or failure.

158th Insight: You are a **DIVINE** power source endowed with a vast reservoir of power.

159th Insight: If you want to change the results you get out of life, change how you think about life.

160th Insight: Life teaches those who are attentive and take heed to life; therefore, those who do not pay attention to life fail to learn from life.

161st Insight: Whatever you think about yourself determines how you feel about yourself, and however you feel about yourself determines how you present yourself to the world.

162nd Insight: Whatever you are or become in life, somewhere along the journey of life, you chose to be or to become by the choices you've made.

163rd Insight: You are beautiful by nature; therefore, capable of manifesting beauty in the world.

164th Insight: A plan without a back-up plan is not a plan, because you have failed to plan.

165th Insight: Creation is a divine plan, on a divine scale, which you are a product thereof. Therefore, act accordingly; conduct your life according to a plan.

166th Insight: You are perfection, perfect by nature, the creation of perfection; thus, rendering you a perfect creation.

167th Insight: The joy of life is having life; therefore, exercise your creativity and make the best of your life (regardless of your situation).

168th Insight: Confusion is the end result of ignorance and clarity is the product of knowledge; therefore, as you grow in knowledge you will begin to see life clearer.

169th Insight: Your mind is revealed and presented within your words; every act of communication discloses not only the contents of your mind but the quality of it as well.

170th Insight: You are your own responsibility; thus, you have been charged with the responsibility of self-management.

171st Insight: Nothing meaningful, of great value or worth, happens instantly, or immediately. There is always a process involved requiring time.

172nd Insight: Destiny isn't fixed; you choose your destiny. You become what you are destined to become by your own choosing.

173rd Insight: You succeed when you choose to succeed. However, your choice must be supported by belief and commitment and reinforced with determined action.

174th Insight: Whatever you get from your situations is determined by how you perceive them.

175th Insight: Structure structures and structure is the key to structured behavior. Therefore, endeavor daily to establish structure.

176th Insight: You are ultimately the master of yourself, endowed with the ability to master self. However, when you fail to maximize this ability you become mastered by something else or someone else.

177th Insight: To be yourself is to know yourself, yet to know yourself is to study yourself. Therefore, studying yourself is essential to being yourself.

178th Insight: Good things does not come to those who wait. Good things come to those who take the initiative to make a good thing happen.

179th Insight: Nothing can really prevent you from succeeding other than you, because you are endowed with the principle of success. You come to the world equipped to succeed.

180th Insight: Nothing external of you possesses power over you, for you are a power source endowed with the power to exercise power over yourself.

181st Insight: Thinking is a habitual function of the mind, which manifests into habitual behavior; therefore, if you change your habit of thinking, you will change your habit of behavior.

182nd Insight: You are as excellent as you excel to be; excellent is determined. You are the determining factor! Excellence is a process not a destination, a constant, not a point reached.

183rd Insight: Obstacles exist only to the degree you perceive them to be. Overcoming them is a matter of not perceiving there existence.

184th Insight: Thinking is boundless, it has no real limits. Therefore, if you expand your thinking capacity beyond what you normally think you can expand your world.

185th Insight: Thought is the ultimate originator, the great initiator of everything.

186th Insight: You are a creator endowed with creative potential to create whatever you creatively conceive.

187th Insight: What is failure other than not attempting to succeed, or attempting to do so yet not succeeding, then quitting.

188th Insight: You can only go as far as you aspire; therefore, if you fail to aspire you will never go anywhere. Aspirations are directional, they compel motion, and thus, they're motivational.

189th Insight: We are essentially the same being, woven together by a divine cosmic tread rendering us one. Thus, the great journey of life concerns itself with the cultivation of the realization of our essential being: oneness.

190th Insight: By virtue of your existence you have purpose; however, the purpose that you serve in life will be determined by what you do in life.

191st Insight: You fail when you choose to fail by not believing you can succeed. Thus, when you don't believe in your ability to come out on top, you end up on the bottom.

192nd Insight: Things change in your life when you change things in your life.

193rd Insight: You win when you commit to winning, and there is no commitment without sacrifice; therefore, winning demands sacrifice.

194th Insight: Your ultimate power is your mind.

195th Insight: You are what you do; therefore, change what you do to change what you are.

196th Insight: Be as you are by being yourself, yet to be yourself is to know yourself; therefore, know yourself so you can be yourself. This requires the study of self!

197th Insight: With the passing of each successive moment of time you're different.

198th Insight: You exist inside and outside of your mind as a unitary part of the Divine mind.

199th Insight: You are the Divine glory of creation; therefore, glory in creation.

200th Insight: Your consequences in life are your choices in life.

201st Insight: You must be what we are by nature: the Truth. Therefore, stop acting falsely thereby being what you are not by nature.

202nd Insight: You are the past, present and future. You decide them all, **NOW**. Therefore, acting in the moment of **NOW** determines the past, present and future.

203rd Insight: History is written NOW, and is forever NOW!

204th Insight: We are only as successful as we conceive and perceive ourselves to being.

205th Insight: "BEING" is in a constant state of flux; therefore, your "BEING" is in a constant state of change; you're constantly changing progressively or regressively.

206th Insight: Pain is the passageway to healing; therefore, to heal is to experience pain.

207th Insight: Being prioritized is the key to maximizing time, and when you maximize time you maximize results.

208th Insight: There is a distinct difference between THINKING and FUNCTIONING. Many are programmed to FUNCTION, while only a few are reared to THINK.

209th Insight: No-one stay as they are, you either progress and develop or regress and deteriorate.

210th Insight: Ignorance is natural to the process of enlightenment. That which is un-natural about ignorance is its denial and refusal to transform it into knowledge.

211th Insight: Communication is a reflection and conveyor of consciousness.

212th Insight: Life is fundamentally simple, ignorance complicates it.

213th Insight: We speak what we are and we are what we speak.

214th Insight: If you do not do for yourself, you do not know what you can do for yourself.

215th Insight: What you understand about yourself determines to what degree you utilize yourself.

216th Insight: Winning must be an internal experience before a manifest reality.

217th Insight: A great idea not worked is a useless idea.

218th Insight: Failure to prepare for success in life is preparation for failure in life.

219th Insight: Ignorance breeds confusion; thus, the greater your ignorance, the greater your confusion.

220th Insight: Knowledge produces clarity; thus, greater your knowledge, greater the degree of your clarity.

221st Insight: One of life's beauties is that it presents you with a myriad of opportunities to maximize your potential.

222nd Insight: What you do with life is determined by what you know and understand about life.

223rd Insight: When you do not understand the value of something you will mis-use it and ultimately abuse it. Therefore, in all your doing seek understanding.

224th Insight: Trials and tribulations, appropriately handled, are the crucible wherein strong and resolute character is forged.

225th Insight: Thought without focus and direction is dangerous; therefore, always focus and direct your thoughts.

226th Insight: Thought without action is useless and action without thought is destructive; thought and action must be linked.

227th Insight: If you do not take charge of your life, your life will be taken charge of.

228th Insight: To fear self-confrontation is to fear changing yourself.

229ᵗʰ Insight: What you do in life will determine who you are in life, and who you are in life is determined by what you do in life.

230ᵗʰ Insight: Life is the prime institution and experience is the master teacher.

231ˢᵗ Insight: Growth and development is forged and fostered; it's not automatic.

232ⁿᵈ Insight: Self-validation is the best validation; seek validation from within not without.

232rd Insight: You are only bound by your thoughts. Think boundlessly and you shall be.

233ʳᵈ Insight: You are a natural being; therefore, the optimal way of life is the natural way.

234ᵗʰ Insight: To be all that you are destine to be, you must accept the challenge of life.

235ᵗʰ Insight: You are as powerful as you truly conceive and believe yourself to be.

236ᵗʰ Insight: The value of experience is determined by the lesson [s] learnt.

237ᵗʰ Insight: If you maintain yourself well you will function well; wellness is a matter of taking care of yourself well.

238ᵗʰ Insight: Do what you say and say only what you can do.

239th Insight: Whatever you do or don't do makes a statement.

240th Insight: Definitions and concepts are powerful, they influence and dictate behavior.

241st Insight: Organized oppression must be counterpoised with an equally organized or superior resistance.

242nd Insight: The central thought of a revolutionary, around which all other thoughts revolve, is revolution. The idea of revolution is the nucleus, the center from which all other thoughts emanate.

243rd Insight: Do not allow yourself to become distracted and consumed by your oppressive state that you fail to plan and strategize for your own liberation.

244th Insight: Oppression is always intentional and intended, never haphazard. Therefore, its demise must be intentional and intended, not wishful thinking.

245th Insight: Growth and development is a consequence of struggle; resistance is inevitable.

246th Insight: There can be no self-progression and advancement without internal contention.

247th Insight: Freedom or the lack thereof is a matter of mind; for you are as free as you can conceive yourself to be and act accordingly so.

248th Insight: The reality of the matter is that you are bound by nothing, for you are endowed with abilities and possess the power to transcend all boundaries.

249th Insight: You are always in contention with yourself, for self-contention is the passageway to liberated thoughts.

250th Insight: Freedom is free to be taken or denied; however, it is your responsibility to secure it for yourself.

251st Insight: To not seek, in some shape, form or fashion, to change your situation or condition is an indication of being content with that situation or condition.

252nd Insight: Productive change requires courage and demands sacrifice.

253rd Insight: If you do not direct yourself against the socio-politico forces at work within society you will be directed by them.

254th Insight: You can be oppressed only as long as you accept oppression.

255th Insight: Never question your instincts; it is the **DIVINE** within communicating to you.

256th Insight: Self-acceptance is a matter of self-knowledge; to accept who you are to avoid pretending to be someone other than yourself requires that you know who you are.

257th Insight: Opportunity presents itself at the most favorable time in your life; however, it's your responsibility to recognize it.

258th Insight: You can only go in life as far as your knowledge will take you.

259th Insight: Adversity and difficult situations will reveal you to yourself.

260th Insight: Think not that you can't because you can. It's just a matter of skill, creativity and WILL.

261st Insight: You are divinely prepared to succeed; however, you must work for success divinely.

262nd Insight: Life challenges you to fully emerge, to rise above circumstances and conditions, to manifest DIVINITY.

263rd Insight: Self competition is the best competition; you are your most formidable competitor.

264th Insight: Your response to life is determined by what you understand about life; therefore, an insufficient response to life is dictated by an insufficient understanding of life.

265th Insight: What you make of your life will be determined by what you understand about your life.

266th Insight: Pursue your goals with great zeal, passion and conviction. To do so is to succeed!

267th Insight: You are not born a thinker; you are born with the potential to think. Thinking is a learnt skill and thinkers are cultivated.

268th Insight: Indiscipline thinking is wondrous thinking and wondrous thinking is reckless behavior.

269th Insight: To develop yourself is to challenge yourself; self-development is self-challenging.

270th Insight: You are part of a purposeful creation, living in a purposeful universe, created for a purpose.

280th Insight: You are charged with the task of taking charge of yourself.

281st Insight: You are endowed with the potential to perpetually evolve.

282nd Insight: He who talks more than he listens and reflects is a fool.

283rd Insight: Information without the discipline to implement it is useless.

284th Insight: Liberation is never haphazardly obtained; you do not stumble onto it by chance. It is gained through protracted planned struggle!

285th Insight: Do not live within the experience of pain, but rather learn from the lessons therein.

286th Insight: To live within the experience of pain is to become hostage to that experience, which thwarts growth and development.

287th Insight: Lessons, although beneficial, aren't necessarily painless.

288th Insight: Universal order is the way that we must emulate.

289th Insight: To avoid struggle is to prolong progress, for progress is forged through struggle.

290th Insight: Growth and development are not automatic; they must be self-directed and guided.

291st Insight: You do not live unto yourself, you live in communion with and as an extension of others; your existence is predicated upon the existence of your ancestors.

292nd Insight: Your life will be as organized as much as you endeavor to organize it.

293rd insight: You behave as you think and you think as you behave.

294th Insight: You will ultimately go where your interest truly is not where you profess it to be.

295th Insight: Your Life is a priority; therefore, your life must be prioritized.

296th Insight: You cannot hope or wish things into existence; you must bring things into existence through the use of your own creative ability.

297th Insight: You will only accomplish in life that which you have a burning desire to accomplish in life.

298th Insight: You will not grasp hold of that which you are not prepared and ready to grasp hold of, it will only elude you.

299th Insight: You are the ultimate definer of your life by what you do or don't do with your life.

300th Insight: Nothing just happens; everything is processional. Situations, circumstances and events are the culmination of a process.

301st Insight: Your path is already chosen, thus, your task is to remember the path you've chosen.

302nd Insight: Enlightenment is arrived at through the passageway of ignorance.

303rd Insight: You must journey through your history to know yourself.

304th Insight: Productive change will be met with internal and external opposition.

305th Insight: Living is the ultimate experience to teach the art of living.

306th Insight: All experiences occur at the right time; your challenge is to make sense of the experience so that you may learn from it.

307th Insight: Nothing is truly complicated; complications arise from ignorance.

308th Insight: Truly believe in your beliefs, therein lies power.

309th Insight: Think critically, speak wisely and walk sincerely.

310th Insight: Oppression, correctly understood, negates leisure. But demands perpetual work.

311th Insight: Self-knowledge is a matter of correct historical connectivity and cultural grounding.

312th Insight: Oppression is a relative state of reality, it is not absolute.

313th Insight: Oppression negates freedom; you cannot exercise freedom (in the truest sense of the word) under oppression.

314th Insight: To be is to struggle, and to struggle is to validate your existence.

315th Insight: Networking facilitates liberation because liberation is a process of networking.

316th Insight: You are purpose filled; your task is to unleash it.

317th Insight: Success is the result of many, not one.

318th Insight: Allegiance cannot be divided, it's 100% or it's not allegiance.

319: Insight: Productive growth and development is not easy; however, it's rewarding.

320th Insight: Living isn't easy, yet that's the beauty of life (struggle). Our struggles shape and fashion us into who and what we are.

321st Insight: Discipline is not something to be detested but rather honored; discipline builds character.

322nd Insight: There's a power in sincerity. To arrive at it will enable you to connect with others that are sincere and detect hypocrites.

323rd Insight: Never content yourself with flaunting information; concern yourself with mastering the art of its application.

324th Insight: Disagreements aren't necessarily bad, intelligent disagreements foster growth.

325th Insight: Organized unity is force; force is power and power is the only force that is recognized and respected.

326th Insight: You can only be what you know; if you know nothing how can you be anything other than nothing.

327th Insight: Divine justice is dispensed within the court realm of your mind; your conscience is the ultimate judge, jury and executioner.

328th Insight: Authentic success is forged; it's not given to you.

329th Insight: You get out of life what you go get out of life.

330th Insight: Culture is the great imperative. To be without culture is equivalent to being without an immune system, which will render you susceptible to all types of psycho-socio-emotional germs and viruses.

331st Insight: The extremes to which you are willing to go to achieve liberation will be determined by your understanding of the importance of liberation.

332nd Insight: You are more than you are.

333rd Insight: You are always what you were, what you are and what you are becoming; of the three, in the final analysis, what you become matters most.

334th Insight: The beauty of growth and development is the passageway of struggle.

335th Insight: You live in history, and all that you do become history; therefore do all that you do to leave an ever lasting impression upon history.

336th Insight: The purpose of experience is to provide you with a lesson, be it favorable or non-favorable; experience is an opportunity to learn.

337th Insight: What you are within the world is what you are within your mind; your actions are a manifestation of your mind.

338th Insight: Liberation necessitates sacrifice; therefore, wherever there's no sacrifice, there can be no liberation.

339th Insight: There is always time to do something because there is always time to do nothing.

340th Insight: Your most important moment in time is NOW; therefore, always make the best use of NOW.

341st Insight: To not value your word is to not value yourself, for your word represents you.

342nd Insight: You are judged by what you do, not by how good you say the things that you say.

343rd Insight: What you say says a lot about you; however, what you do reveals who you are.

344th Insight: How you present yourself is often times how you are judged; therefore, make sure you always present yourself well organized and neat.

345th Insight: Talking without thinking is foolish.

346th Insight: What seems to be is rarely what it seems to be.

347th Insight: To think and not act is useless, whereas, to act and not think is reckless.

348th Insight: It is not good to be into everything because you cannot be good at everything.

349th Insight: You are the ultimate definer of your life by what you do or don't do with your life.

350th Insight: Time waits for no-one and loss time can't be recovered; therefore, master the use of time.

351st Insight: What you don't do matters, it is equally important as what you do.

352nd Insight: The quality of your system will determine the quality of your product.

353rd Insight: Consistency + resistance foster development.

354th Insight: Love nurtures and develops; whereas, anger, resentment and self-pity inhibits nurturing and thwarts development.

355th Insight: To "BE" all that you are destine to "BE" you must embrace all that you are.

356th Insight: Receive only what you are truly deserving of and accept only what you can handle.

357th Insight: Your value can be measured by what you value.

358th Insight: What you feel is always real; however, this doesn't mean your interpretation of what you feel is always accurate.

359th Insight: If you do not understand the value of time it's virtually impossible to understand the true value of life.

360th Insight: You cannot give to another what you do not possess yourself.

Section four
The Ideal

The UrBan Philosopher

An UrBan Philosopher is someone who engages him or herself in the process of deliberate thought, who never stop thinking, who dare to think. An UrBan Philosopher is a conceptualizer; a great thinker. Thus, his or her greatness, as a great thinker, is arrived at through a process of meditation, reflection and critical assessment. An UrBan Philosopher is a practitioner of deep thought. Therefore, the thoughts of an UrBan Philosopher are forever under-going a process of transmutation, only to continuously crystallize into an organized set of thoughts more acute than they previously were. An UrBan Philosopher clearly understands that his or her thoughts must be systematically honed (constantly)! The activity of thinking, to an UrBan Philosopher, is an art she or he seeks to master. A progressive and proactive thinker is what he is; therefore, progressive and proactive thinking is what she practices. He or she challenges him or herself, constantly analyzing and evaluating his or her present mode-of-thought, discarding all incorrect, obsolete and non-applicable ideas.

An UrBan Philosopher engages in critical thinking, as a discipline, on a daily basis, to train her or his thoughts, to function in a specific mode. Through the diligent practice of such, the thought process of an UrBan Philosopher operates at a capacity above and beyond average. An UrBan Philosopher is a problem solver; he or she is solution oriented. He is analytical, evaluative and thorough, constantly looking and searching, critically and diligently for answers. By extension, an UrBan Philosopher is a calculated thinker. Thus, objective and systematic reasoning are always applied prior to executing any of his or her actions. The art of thinking must be mastered; therefore, the process of critical thinking must be practiced. This necessarily includes the practice of theorizing, conceptualizing, contemplating, introspection, strategizing and synthesizing. The idea of elevating your thought process must be a daily sought after goal.

To be an UrBan Philosopher demands that you always think of how to excel yourself, how to advance upon your present level of awareness and how to perfect your craft, function or profession. You can never be lax in the area of critical thinking (which doesn't mean a bunch of random jammed up thoughts but well selected, sorted out and structured thoughts)! Concentrated and bridled thoughts are the way of the UrBan Philosopher! The organization of thoughts is indispensable to mastering the art of thinking, because only organized thoughts are acute, potent and penetrating. Furthermore, only organized and structured thoughts are incisive and decisive thoughts. This is what facilitates calculated thinking, and calculated thinking breeds calculated actions.

An UrBan Philosopher is a social tactician and strategist; he or she interact with and engage human beings tactfully, thus, her or his behavior is always guided by tactic and strategy. Random and empty actions are guarded against at all cost. He or she never executes an action for the sake of it: an UrBan Philosopher always moves with purpose, according to a plan and design. Even the necessity of improvisation is pre-factored into the equation of an UrBan Philosopher's mode-of-execution; for he or she knows that un-foreseen events often occur. Therefore, an UrBan Philosopher always executes his or her plans with caution, preparing to improvise. Improvisation is inherent within an UrBan Philosopher's mode-of-execution; the thought of improvisation pervades the thinking of an UrBan Philosopher. He or she thinks to improvise and improvises to think, always ready to shift, redirect or re-focus his or her execution strategy. The art of *maneuverability*, *adaptability* and *flexibility* are essential qualities of an UrBan Philosopher; thus, fluidity is the way of an UrBan Philosopher. Not rigidity! Therefore, the ability to skillfully improvise is indispensable to the make-up of an UrBan Philosopher.

An UrBan Philosopher endeavors daily to never get caught off guard; he or she suspects everything to happen and expects anything to occur, and plans accordingly. Knowing plans very rarely go according to plan, he or she is never surprised by the slight divergence or disruption of a plan caused by the un-predictable reality of an unforeseen occurrence. He or she is impervious to this kind of surprise! Whenever mishaps and misfortune befalls an UrBan Philosopher, he or she is never distracted or derailed. Neither does he despair nor is she dismayed by the manifestation of unfavorable events. Set-backs are expected and prepared for!

Worrying is not an option either, by doing so fractures concentration and shatters focus. It diverts attention from the immediate task at hand; therefore, an UrBan Philosopher holds course, forever determined to succeed. There is a continued march forward to achieve the sought after goals and objectives; never stopping to languish in self-defeat. Thus, an UrBan Philosopher always exercises resiliency and perseverance.

Crucial to the make-up of an UrBan Philosopher is the capacity to forever push forward against tumultuous odds; to envision success and become it. She or he is always calm, cool and collected in the face of difficulty or adversity; never complaining, irate or outwardly manifesting frustration, yet maintaining a great degree of composure, while forever demonstrating the mental and psychological capacity to remain stable and focused; never losing sight of his or her ultimate objective: *Self-mastery in pursuit of supreme-discipline.* Forever challenging self; endeavoring daily to outstrip self, for self is the most formidable component. Self-discipline is the ideal reality, for through self-discipline self-mastery is possible. Self-mastery is the apex of human perfection, which is the ideal state of being. However, this is a perpetual pursuit. The journey of human perfectibility is an arduous yet rewarding path. It's a life-time journey! Nevertheless, travelling such a path (which has to be a willful and conscious choice) enhances and refines your being as long as you are on the path. Thus, the longer you are on the path the closer you are to human perfectibility.

The idea of human perfectibility is not idealistic or farfetched; human actions and behavior are perfect in the sense that they are aligned with and correspond to universal law and divine order. When the actions and behavior are in sync, harmonized and balanced with the universal scheme of things they are perfect. Perfect to the degree they are fluid and flow with the divine rhythm of the universe; they are not interfering with, disrupting, detracting from, obstructing or hindering the natural universal flow of energy. For the natural flow and universal order of the universe is perfect; this means the divine laws that oversee, regulate and govern all things are perfect. Perfect is the universe! The cosmic essence underlying reality is perfect. Therefore, when human actions and behavior align and comport with the divine laws and universal order of the universe, they're perfect. This does not preclude mistakes, for mistakes are a necessary part of the process of human perfectibility.

Mistakes are teaching moments for an UrBan Philosopher; they are life lessons. They afford her the opportunity to learn from self by studying and analyzing her own behavior, to ultimately perfect her behavior. Mistakes aren't imperfection. This concept of imperfection is crippling, in that, it breeds a mentality that justifies and makes excuses for mediocrity: laxness, procrastination, dereliction, listless, incompetence, laziness, dis-organization and failure. The universe is perfection by design and creation, and we are apart of the universe, not separate from it; therefore, we are apart its perfection. What we are by nature is the quality of our perfection; thus, we are endowed with and possess the ability to give full expression to our perfect nature. Our challenge and task is to tap into, cultivate and manifest the essence of our nature---to be what we are by nature---DIVINE BEINGS.

As long as we buy into and accept this notion of our inherent imperfectability, we can never and will never rise above our current state of social-emotional, politico-economic and psycho-spiritual decadence and deterioration. These will persist until we awaken the DIVINE within and give it full expression. DIVINITY is perfect and we are DIVINE; therefore, we are perfect. Knowing is doing; thus, since we do not know we are DIVINE, we do not do DIVINE things. We do not act DIVINELY because we have been made ignorant of our DIVINITY. Our thought & practice (our behavior) does not reflect our essence because we do not know our essence.

We are our essence. However, we must awaken to the knowledge of our essence in order to manifest our essence. Therefore, we must learn to embrace and accept our Africanity. This requires of us to increase and enhance our study of authentic African history & culture. For within our culture is the knowledge of who we are by nature and within our history are the examples of how we are to be; how to behave in accord with our nature to manifest our essence. As we deepen our knowledge and broaden our awareness of who and what we are by nature, we subsequently move closer towards our nature, and the closer we move towards our nature is the closer we are moving towards perfection. This will not and cannot be achieved while in a state of ignorance, disbelief, denial and/or doubt.

Our earthly sojourn is a DIVINE process. Although replete with chaos, confusion, corruption, negativity and destruction etc., we must journey along this earthly path to regain our original state of perfection---peaceful-stillness. We have falling from this state of being and allowed ourselves to become intoxicated; thereby, addicted to the carnal desires of this world. Thus, we have forgotten who and what we are by nature; therefore, we do not know we are perfect beings. We have been made ignorant of our perfect essence, and in the final analysis, we are what we are in essence.

An UrBan Philosopher is a healer; an UrBan Therapist (there are enough destroyers in the world). An UrBan Therapist is internally composed; he or she possesses a unique intellectual-emotional blend. That's why UrBan Therapy is the act of administering to the socio-emotional-psycho-spiritual and cultural needs of African people, to facilitate healing. Thus, to develop social competence, cultivate emotional stability, foster psychological soundness, and engender spiritual attunement and awareness.

UrBan Therapy is a function of UrBan Philosophy that places a particular focus and emphasis on the socio-emotional-psycho-spiritual needs of African people. UrBan Therapy by definition is Liberation Therapy. The primary objective of which is: freeing African people from the socio-emotional-psycho-spiritual and cultural fetters that interferes with, obstructs and disrupts healthy human interaction, impedes productive social practices and stifles spiritual development. In short these fetters suppress the over-all evolution of African people. They are:

- **Psychological instability**
- **Social incompetence**
- **Emotional-underdevelopment**
- **Spiritual stagnation**
- **Cultural disorientation**

UrBan Therapy is a philosophical-therapeutic process, rooted in an African context, designed to administer to the psycho-social needs, foster the emotional development and cultivate the spiritual awareness of African people to facilitate intra-personal, interpersonal and intra-group socio-emotional-psycho-spiritual healing. The resources, references, tools of analysis, evaluative measures and experiences utilized are all African. Therefore, UrBan Therapy posits African culture as the instructive, operative and corrective principle in the cultivation, enhancement and enrichment of healthy and wholesome behavior for African people.

UrBan Therapy rest upon the following three premises:

1st Premise:

- The socio-emotional-psycho-spiritual fetters (psychological instability, social incompetence, emotional under-development & spiritual stagnation) interfering with and obstructing productive human interaction and engagement among African people are due to a lack of African culture (there is a cultural void).

2nd Premise:

- The dysfunctional and maladaptive behaviors displayed by African people (not all) are the result of cultural dis-orientation, which breeds cultural confusion, cultural dis-placement and cultural delusion. These facilitate cultural assimilation (absorbed into and subsequently influenced by an alien cultural system). This in turn leads to inter-personal, intra-personal and intra-group incapacitation.

3rd **Premise:**

- The underlying factor concerning socio-emotional-psycho-spiritual health, wellness and wholeness is African culture. Therefore these can only be effectively remedied through the correct study, internalization and practice of authentic African history and culture. African culture is the great imperative for African people. Thus, African culture is indispensable to the holistic health of African people.

An UrBan Philosopher is a Social Reformer seeking social reformation for African people yet radical progress. In this sense, an UrBan Philosopher is a revolutionary. He or she has dedicated his or her entire existence to the radical yet productive transformation of the socio-politico-economic conditions of African people. He endeavors earnestly to effect progressive change within the African world; never rash or haste in movement, never impulsive, and he never underestimates (or over-estimates for that matter) the oppressor. He is never the aggressor in any shape, form or fashion. However, in the event of transgression (such as oppression) he will fight until the eradication of the transgression.

An UrBan Philosopher is a Vanguard of African people: disciplined, observant, knowledgeable, prepared; astute in judgment and is on the forefront to facilitate African victory: sovereignty. She understands the benefit of collective work and responsibility; therefore, strives to perfect it. United forces prosper and advance, while competitive oppositions (internal strife) suffer and wither away. This is un-characteristic of UrBan Philosophical behavior! There's unity, respect, trust, loyalty and faith amongst revolutionaries. A revolutionary is level-headed, not driven by blind-anger and mis-directed frustration. These if not properly channeled often leads to destruction.

A revolutionary is not born overnight; she has selectively conditioned herself or has been shaped by life's experiences. Every aspect of her makeup has been thoroughly examined then placed into proper context within the structure of her character. This means weaknesses are strengthened and strengths enhanced. There is on-going self-development work in the midst of struggle; for the revolutionary is a product in motion not an end. Therefore, an UrBan Philosopher is forever perfecting herself to perfect her function as an UrBan Philosopher: to enhance and refine the thought process of African people; to add a new dynamic to human thought and reasoning.

In conclusion, the process of becoming an UrBan Philosopher involves disciplined thoughts. For in order to be an UrBan Philosopher you have to be able to exercise control over your thoughts; you have to be in control of you. This requires the exercise of great mental concentration, reflection, deliberation, composure, equilibrium, determination and self-knowledge. Therefore, you have to possess the ability to organize your thoughts according to a specific line-of-reasoning. Your thinking has to be under your control! Thus, the cultivation and development of acute, incisive, decisive and critical thinking can only be realized through a function of systematized thoughts.

The Seven Cardinal Virtues of UrBan Philosophy

The seven cardinal virtues of UrBan Philosophy are points of concerns or rather principles of interest of an UrBan Philosopher. Therefore, great concern and focused interest is given to each one. In fact, they are internal functions of an UrBan Philosopher. These internal functions are extremely important; therefore, fundamental to an UrBan Philosopher's over-all constitution. An UrBan Philosopher is: discipline, humility, tenacity, creativity, studious, self-knowledge and courage. These are what an UrBan Philosopher endeavors daily to cultivate and practice.

Discipline:
- An UrBan Philosophy endeavors daily to master self-discipline in the pursuit of supreme discipline. An UrBan Philosopher is proactive. He or she strives to exemplify self-control and orderliness, to execute fortitude, to remain steadfast and maintain a strong resolve in the face of oppression.

Humility:
- An UrBan Philosophy endeavors daily to master humility through the continued display of humbleness in the service of African people. She or he is always humble; therefore, forever on guard against arrogance. Self-security and self-honesty are dominating traits of an UrBan Philosopher's character.

Tenacity:
- An UrBan Philosopher endeavors daily to practice tenacity in the face of oppression. An UrBan Philosopher is Consistent and resilient. He or she recovers fast from setbacks or defeats; and is persistent in the pursuit of African sovereignty (never giving up). This is a perpetual pursuit.

Creativity:

- An UrBan Philosopher endeavors daily to demon-strate creativity in pursuit of African sovereignty. An UrBan Philosopher is inventive and innovative in the face of oppression. Creativity is inextricably bound up in UrBan Philosophy.

Studious:

- An UrBan Philosopher endeavors daily to remain studious in search of ways to defeat oppression to realize African sovereignty. An UrBan Philosopher is a perpetual student. He or she is an industrious per-son and very diligent in his or her prosecution of the African Liberation Struggle.

Self-knowledge:

- An UrBan Philosopher endeavors daily to cultivate and practice self-knowledge in the service of African peo-ple. Self-knowledge enables an UrBan Philosopher to perform and conduct him or herself well within the African Liberation Struggle (to adhere to high mor-als and sound principles). An UrBan Philosopher is refined and enhanced through self-knowledge.

Courage:

- An UrBan Philosopher endeavors daily to exemplify courage, by doing the right thing whenever time, cir-cumstances and conditions dictates the necessity of doing the right thing. The right thing in this context is determined by African morality (a life-centered morality). An UrBan Philosopher is an implacable freedom fighter, in the service of African people, guided by Ma'at.

Section five
The Laws

Tri-Laws *Of* **Wisdom**

UrBan Philosophy holds that wisdom is a developmental process of insight, prudence, keen awareness, humility, foresight, hind-sight and understanding (cultivated and produced thru time). Moreover, we hold that wisdom is the realization of a heightened perceptive aptitude! By extension, wisdom is a self-learnt process of enlightenment, developing and deepening in time, with time. Therefore, wisdom cannot be taught, nor is wisdom an end in itself (it is not a conclusion). Neither is wisdom static. It is not a point to be reached or arrived at; it is a process. Wisdom is enhanced and refined thru and by practice. Thus, wisdom sharpens itself in time and evolves with time. Time affords one the opportunity to experience and observe a multitude of things, to live life, which one can examine, deliberate on and reflect upon. This is indispensable to the process of wisdom.

1st Law
I don't know anything except I need to know

The wise does not profess to know anything. However, the wise is acutely aware of the need to know, to search for right-knowledge and cultivate enlightenment. The realization of this need is the beginning of wisdom. For it is a display of modesty and an act of honesty (two attributes of wisdoms). Both of which are indispensable to and facilitates the process of progressive learning, the passageway to wisdom. There is a perpetual need to learn in pursuit of knowing.

2nd Law
With the acquisition of information, humble yourself even more

To increase in knowledge should cause you to humble yourself. For each acquisition of information should reveal to you how much you do not know. This revelation should engender humility, to guard against arrogance, because arrogance doesn't allow any room for growth and development. Nor does it make possible the realization of wisdom. Arrogance disrupts and obstructs the passageway to wisdom. Thus, an arrogant person is an unwise person.

3rd Law
Seek wisdom thru the diligent study of experience

Wisdom is a social product, a process cultivated and developed thru the careful study and examination of years of cumulative experiences. For therein lie the instructive lessons. Only when the lessons are extracted from experience, incorporated into our lives and applied to our approach to life is wisdom developed and evolved. Learning from the lessons inherent in experience is crucial to the cultivation and development of wisdom. This can only be done thru and by the diligent study of experience (indirect or direct). Experience avails nothing to those who fail to learn from it.

The Fundamental Laws *Of* Power

All phenomena adhere to and are governed by their own set of laws. Power, as a type of phenomena, is not exempt from this rule. It, too, is governed by a unique set of laws. And it is these laws that defines and determines the nature of the power. The laws oversee its development and dictate its execution. This is not an attempt to define power (that has already been done by Dr. Wade Nobles). This is merely an elaboration of the laws governing power; the laws regulating how it is manifested.

1st
The Law of Disciplined Thought:

The human capacity to achieve, express and manifest power is highly dependent upon one's ability to exercise and execute disciplined thought, which is a function of a structured and organized mind. Thought is a mental process that can be mastered and controlled to maximize its function. Thus, thought is the decisive factor in human society. A focused and un-distracted mind is crucial to the cultivation of incisive and decisive thoughts, which are essential to the manifestation of power.

2nd
The Law of Conceptual Aptitude:

The exercise of conceptual ability and performance is instrumental in the process of expressed-power. The power dynamic as it manifests and takes shape is contingent upon conceptual aptitude. Therefore, the ability to conceive and bring into existence quality concepts is indispensable to the manifestation of power. Conceptual thinking is inextricably tied to power. Power as we know it and understand it has its origin within a conceptual seed. Power isn't birthed from nothing; power doesn't just happen. Power is conceived! There can be no actual manifestation of power without a conceptual manifestation of power. Thus, the inability to conceive of power will obstruct one's ability to manifest power.

3rd
The Law of Visual Aptitude:

The ability to see beyond the now into the now-to-be; to envision realities not-yet manifest is inextricably bound up in the power dynamic. Thus, clear and precise vision; penetrating internal vision, is indispensable to power. Visual aptitude is crucial to the exercise and maintenance of power. Power has to be envisioned; it has to be conceptually clear within the mind, not mentally murky. The manifestation of power must be perceived before the actual manifestation of power. Thus the manifestation of power if highly dependent upon visual aptitude; the ability to envision a reality before materializes.

4th
The Law Execution:

Power must be carried through to fruition. Power must be manifested. Power doesn't just happen; power must be made to happen. Power must be done. It involves doing to bring about desired results. Power must be executed! Thus, the ability to execute a plan-of-action with confidence and resolve is essential to the act of power. Power isn't static; it's dynamic! Therefore, power must be acted upon. The power dynamic must be carried into practice.

5th
The Law of Will:

Self-motivation is indispensable to the power dynamic. The execution necessary to the manifestation of power must be self-initiated. The drive and push to manifest power must originate internally. Thus, the faculty of Will is the force and power behind execution. It's that determined determination; the resiliency and the perseverance to manifest power. This is what makes execution possible! The great push and constant push to execute power is Will. Power cannot be wished into existence, power must be "Willed" into existence

Section six

The Success Factor

DEPS

DEPS is an attitude of mind. It is the ability to push forward against all odds. It's audacity on top of audacity; an intense yearning to succeed; to not quit, to not give up or give in to setbacks. It is the capacity to surmount the seemingly un-surmountable. It's that special something that ignite and set your soul ablaze; it is that internal fire, concentrated energy. It is that *it* thing! Will-power plus drive plus focus! DEPS is rooted in four **(4)** basic principles. These principles are the cornerstone to success.

- **Desire** is the root to accomplishment. You must possess a burning **desire** to succeed. Thus, to accomplish your goals you must have a strong enough **desire** to do so. If your desire is strong enough you can prevail against all odds. Determination is essential here!

- **Endurance** is the energy necessary to succeed. You must possess the ability to withstand and **endure** minor, and possibly, major setbacks. You must be able to hold on and **endure** in the face of adversity, re-group and continue pursuing your goals. Perseverance and resilience are demanded in this regard!

- **Patience** is the self-willed resolution to forbear and await the realization of success. You must **patiently** pursue your goals with tolerance and moderation. Exercise circumspection and never execute any rash decisions, yet forever remain **patient**. **Patience** is essential to succeeding. Self-control is required in this respect!

- **Sacrifice** is the foundation to success. You must know when and how to **sacrifice** to accomplish your goals. **Sacrifice** is indispensable to accomplishing anything; all accomplishments rest upon **sacrifice.** Therefore, accomplishing your goals demand you give up something or deny yourself something to succeed. Self-discipline is essential here!

Success factors to consider:
- Success is an attitude of mind.
- Success is a behavior orientation.
- Success is determined.
- Success is immaterial.
- Success is a productive state of being.
- Success is the ability to empower another.
- Success is not money or material possessions.
- Success is not status or repute.
- Success is processional, not an end.
- Success is perpetual progression.

10-principles of Success:
- Know and perfect your craft.
- Know what you want.
- Believe in yourself.
- Be determined.
- Never quit.
- Learn from your mistakes.
- Develop a strategy.
- Make it happen.
- Recognize opportunity.
- Stay focused.

Understanding the ten factors of success and applying the ten principles of success are indispensable to a successful life. Success is something you learn to do; it is something you become as oppose to something that is achieved. You cannot taste it, feel it or smell it for that matter; you can only do it, by being it. Success is what you are! However, the criterion of success is how what you are empower and advance what others are. Therefore, your existence must serve to enhance and elevate the existence of others. This is success!

Affirming
Self

Affirming-self are UrBan Philosophical affirmations for self-empowerment. They should be recited daily.

1: I am my greatest challenge and ultimate competitor.

2: I am my motivation.

3: I am my success and my failure.

4: I am the end result of all that I do or don't do.

5: I am whatever I desire enough.

6: I am all that I think.

7: I am all that I think I am.

8: I am more than I am.

9: I am my own limitation.

10: I am my own constitution.

11: I am all that my ancestors were.

12: I am the marvel of the universe.

13: I am my own source of power.

14: I am unique.

15: I am greatness.

Section seven

Ideological System

Scientific Pan-Africanism

Scientific Pan-Africanism starts from a double premise: **1)** African people, everywhere, share a common historical-cultural experience, and **2)** African people, everywhere, belong to a worldwide African community, despite geographical differences, sharing a common socio-politico-economic plight. Therefore, African people are contending with a common enemy: the twin evil of oppression and exploitation. This evil manifest itself as the following systems of dominance: white supremacy (racism), imperialism, capitalism, colonialism, neocolonialism, fascism, sexism, classism and new-age domestic colonialism. Thus, Scientific Pan-Africanism, in an offensive-defense against European systems of dominance, in a proactive effort to preserve the integrity of the Pan-African community, seeks the destruction of the previously mentioned systems. "The society we seek to build among black people, then, is not a capitalistic one. It is a society in which the spirit of community and humanistic love prevail." (Toure, 1965)

The entire thought process and behavior orientation of Scientific Pan-Africanism grows out of the general understanding of the socio-politico-economic plight of African people and their historical-cultural connection. Scientific Pan-Africanism holds: in order to liberate an oppressed people one must have a general understanding of the psyche of the oppressed. An in-depth study of African history and culture will prove to be of great value in this regard. "I address the need for an awakening of African people with an emphasis on the fact that this awakening can occur only through a systematic study of our own rich cultural heritage." (Hilliard, 1997) Thus, Scientific Pan-Africanism is therapeutic. By extension, it's preventive, corrective and instructive. With that in mind, Scientific Pan-Africanism is politically correct and ideologically clear. The purpose of which is to: 1) address and remedy the socio-politico and economic ills plaguing the Pan-African community, 2) aid in the progression of human society and 3) provide a systematic framework to Pan-African thought and practice.

The reformation, restoration and redemption of the Pan-African community are some of the objectives of Scientific Pan-Africanism. This means that Scientific Pan-Africanism is pro-Africa. It's an African ideological-system of liberation; a liberatory thought and praxis. Due to its humanistic quality, Scientific Pan-Africanism is against and loathes injustice across the board. However, Scientific Pan-Africanism was not conceptualized to address the issues of other cultural groups. Our primary concern has to be addressing the issues plaguing the Pan-African community. Therefore, the psychological liberation, and politico-economic empowerment of the Pan-African community is the central focus of the proponents of Scientific Pan-Africanism. "The recovery of political sovereignty is merely one aspect of the question. Economic sovereignty is another. Psychic autonomy is yet another. All three must combine in a dynamic renovative effort." (Diop, 1986)

The psychological liberation and politico-economic empowerment of the Pan-African community will necessarily involve and include the task of unifying and mobilizing African people to take part in their own liberation. However, we mustn't overlook the fact that, "... to have unity it is also necessary to struggle." (Amilcar Cabral, 1973) The struggle for self-determination is a protracted struggle. "We should never lose sight of the fact that the restoration of the cultural personality of African and black peoples in general can only be achieved through struggle." (Diop, 1986) UrBan Philosophy states the following concerning unification and mobilization:

> Unifying is a systematic process consisting of two (2) fundamental Components: 1) establishing and instituting coordinated efforts and 2) cultivating a genuine working togetherness.

It further states:

> Mobilizing is the systematic cultivation of an active sense of group preparedness, a state of readiness, to execute a strategic operation.

Scientific Pan-Africanism is firmly rooted in the evolutionary experience of the worldwide African community. It is the logical consequence of the systematic oppression of African people; thus, consistent with the old adage **"oppression breeds resistance"**. Therefore, Scientific Pan-Africanism is a conscious and purposeful ideological-system of organized resistance. UrBan Philosophy holds that: *organized oppression must be counterpoised with an equally organized or superior resistance.* This point is fundamental to the liberation of the Pan-African community. Scientific Pan-Africanism is an organized system of thought, analysis and practice, governed by a set of scientific laws. As a social philosophy and political ideology, Scientific Pan-Africanism is not a set of incoherent and incongruent ideas haphazardly woven together. On the contrary, Scientific Pan-Africanism is a well thought out organized system of thought and praxis (concepts, tenets, virtues, precepts, laws, aims, and objectives) that has been evolving and perfecting itself for well over 200 years. "The concept Pan-Africanism is not new. It found its expression in African revolts during slavery, and reached its organizational level in the early part of the twentieth century". (Toure, 1965)

Thus, P. Olisanwuche Esedebe (1980) correctly points out:

> Of course, the term *Pan-African* and its derivative *Pan-Africanism* were not coined at the time the phenomenon they describe emerged. (pp. 7)

He continues:

> Though the words *Pan-African and Pan-Africanism* became popular after the 1900 London congress, their substance had been thought out long before. (pp. 7)

Tajudeen Abdul-Raheem (1996) had the following to offer concerning this point:

...while the years 1900 and 1919 can confidently be cited as important reference points for the Pan-African movement, the movement stretches much farther into the distant history of our people. (pp. 1)

Considering the fact Pan-Africanism stretches so far back into our past, it's incumbent upon Pan-African leaders to build upon its foundation to take it to new heights; to further its development and evolve it. This is the challenge of Pan-Africanists in the 21st century. We must stand on the shoulders of our Pan-African predecessors, and push Pan-Africanism to its logical conclusion: Scientific Pan-Africanism. Thus, in his book, Pan- Africanism or Communism, George Padmore (1956) states the following:

In their struggles to attain self-government and self-determination, the younger leaders of Pan-Africanism have the task of building upon the ideological foundation laid by Dr. DuBois, the father of Pan-Africanism.

...They are under the necessity to evolve new political means and organizational techniques adapted to African traditions and circumstances. (pp.19)

Scientific Pan-Africanism is consistent with the theoretical thinking and conceptual framework of *Padmore*. For it is the systematic practice of integrating and synthesizing the philosophies, methodologies and ideological perspectives of Pan-African practitioners. It seeks to demonstrate continuity of thought. By extension, Scientific Pan-Africanism is the evolution and culmination of Pan-African thought and practice. Thus, Scientific Pan-Africanism is Pan-Africanism raised and elevated to a higher level. It is the process by which Pan-Africanism is systematized. This doesn't mean it's not Pan-Africanism or that it's a deviation or detraction from Pan-African thought and practice. On the contrary, Scientific Pan-Africanism adds to and further develops the theoretical framework of Pan-Africanism. Therefore, Scientific Pan-Africanism is an ideological-system of liberation. Speaking on the topic of ideology Kwame Toure (1965) made the following observation:

> In order for the black community to come together we must find a common ideology. (pp. 191)

He continues:

> Any ideology seeking to solve the problems of the African people must find its roots in Pan-Africanism. (pp. 221)

Pan-Africanism is the way! Fundamental to its thought and practice is an active recognition and genuine embracement of the worldwide African community and a sincere commitment to its unification, empowerment and liberation. Pan-Africanism posits that African people have a collective identity and a shared historical consciousness. Moreover, Pan-Africanism embraces and seeks to preserve the total African experience: history and culture. "Pan-Africanists study the history of Africa and her people." (Toure, 1965) This necessarily involves the therapeutic process of **Sankofa.** "The only agenda that will ensure our renewal is SANKOFA." (Hilliard, 1997) Authentic Pan-Africanism encompasses everything African and recognizes only an African people, whom have a common enemy throughout the world. Here's what two of our greats had to say on this matter: "Africans today, irrespective of geographical location, have a common enemy and face common problems." (Toure, 1965) And, "The problems facing the Black societies are essentially the same..." (Diop, 1986)

Scientific Pan-Africanism is consonant in practice and comport with the aforementioned position: it's the logical outgrowth therefrom. Thus, Scientific Pan-Africanism is the continuity and transition of Pan-Africanism; however, Pan-Africanism nonetheless. The word *"Scientific"* prefixed to Pan-Africanism denotes the following *"systematized knowledge derived from observation, study, and experimentation."* Therefore, the word *"Scientific"* does not render it anything other than Pan-Africanism: whatever holds true for one holds true for the other. They are identical, sustained by the same revolutionary current: genuine love for the worldwide African community, sincere commitment to African empowerment and dedication to the eradication of oppression and exploitation.

Scientific Pan-Africanism is the reawakening and the revitalization of Pan-African thought and practice. The unique thing of which is: it's rooted in the grassroots and adapted to the socio-politico climate of the new millennium. Its strength, vigor and potency derive from the African experience and its African orientation. Thus, Scientific

Pan-Africanism incorporates and embodies African spirituality as a fundamental component of its systematic construction. Therefore, we must relinquish the religions of the invaders of Africa. Scientific Pan-Africanism holds: we must return to the spiritual practices of our ancestors to recreate the African personality. This can only be achieved through embracing, internalizing and practicing African culture. African culture is essential to the wholeness and wellness of African people. Thus, "The cultural personality of Africa is inseparable from the restoration of our collective historical consciousness." (Diop, 263)

We prefix *"Scientific"* to Pan-Africanism to serve as a signature mark to distinguish it from pseudo-pan-Africanism. *"Scientific"* sets it apart from everything un-Pan-Africanism and symbolize its originality. Moreover, *"Scientific"* signify and establish the fact that Pan-Africanism, as a system of thought and practice, is a science. Proponents of Scientific Pan-Africanism recognize that Pan-Africanism has been empirically tested and validated, through and by the life and works of true Pan-Africanist. Thus, we deduce five **(5)** fundamental laws from their example: **1)** intimate identification with Africa; **2)** recognition of a worldwide African community; **3)** genuine love for the unification, redemption and empowerment of African people; **4)** African-centered worldview and **5)** a nationalistic orientation. However, due to the development and evolution of Pan-African thought, and the confusion surrounding it, we deduce a sixth **(6)** law: a true practitioner of African cultural norms.

Concerning culture, Dr. Kwame Nkrumah (1963) espoused the following:

…we should nurture our own culture and history if we are to develop that African personality which must provide the educational and intellectual foundations of our Pan-African future. (pp. 49)

The study, understanding and practice of African history and culture is a therapeutic process indispensable to Pan-African liberation. It is essential to the social-emotional and psycho-spiritual healing necessary to reconstruct the African personality. Thus, "The healing process for people of African descent can only be initiated as a consequence of our engagement in deep thought." (Hilliard, 1997) Therefore, African cultural awareness and connectivity is crucial to the cultivation and development of the African spirit. African culture nurtures and nourishes our Africanity.

Scientific Pan-Africanism, as an applied science, holds firm to the scientific principle of integrating theory with practice: the systematic process of implementing theoretical knowledge, against concrete conditions, to transform such knowledge into practical knowledge, from which new insights can derive, to further develop the theory. "There should be no non-theoretical practitioners, and there should be no non-practical theoreticians" (Hilliard, 1997) The truth of any theory is arrived at through a process of trial and error; kinks and glitches can only be discovered and ironed out in practice. Social theory must be connected to social practice. This is the only avenue through which to discover its effectiveness. Theory disconnected from practice is useless. We must test, in practice, through a system of direct action, the socio-politico theory of the unification, redemption and empowerment of African people

On that final point, Chiekh Anta Diop elaborated the following position:

> ...we must have a heightened awareness of the nature of the work to be done, of the efforts to be undertaken... To solve problems by organizing the work...What is important is the organization of the work...We must be armed to the teeth with science to go to re-conquer our cultural inheritance. (pp. 237)

He further states:

> We must stop being dilettantes, dabbling here and there, and become well trained, pluri-disciplinary specialists. (pp. 239)

Scientific Pan-Africanism is consistent with the above quote, for it holds: "Study is a requirement of our redemption." (Hilliard, 1997) Therefore, the proponents of Scientific Pan-Africanism must: 1) "read history incessantly" (Garvey, 1987), and 2) equip themselves, through study, with a broad base of African-centered knowledge. We feel "...that the historian's educational background must be vast and profound." (Diop, 1986) Thus, Scientific Pan-Africanism advances, "No African should be granted leadership in the African community who has not been certified through education or experience as African-centered in consciousness, identity and orientation." (Wilson, 1998) Pan-Africanists must be well studied, and firmly rooted in African history and culture. "Study is important because it is the only way that we can become mentally, spiritually and physically free." (Hilliard, 1997)

Scientific Pan-Africanism is both, political ideology and social philosophy. Moreover, Scientific Pan-Africanism is an economic system, a liberatory pedagogy, and spiritual practice. Therefore, Scientific Pan-Africanism speaks to a distinct mental disposition and behavioral orientation rooted in an authentic African reality. Scientific Pan-Africanism is an African worldview. It was conceptualized in the spirit and interest of the Pan-African community. This renders Scientific Pan-Africanism a direct action ideology and philosophy. It can only find meaning and validity through direct action. The value and worth of any social philosophy or political ideology is determined by the results, or the lack thereof, rendered through a system of direct action. "Any action, regardless of its motives, is sterile unless it produces practical and concrete results." (Cabral, 1973)

Scientific Pan-Africanism is a practical result in that it is the evolution and elevation of Pan-African thought and practice, developed against a background of political transgression and economic exploitation. Thus, Scientific Pan-Africanism is a political ideology of redemption and a social philosophy of restoration. "Man's mission is creation. African renaissance, black renaissance, is inseparable from the restoration of the black world's creativity." (Diop, 1986) Therefore, Scientific Pan-Africanism is the product of African genius and creativity. Moreover, Scientific Pan-Africanism is the political, ideological, philosophical, and cultural clarity necessary for the empowerment of African people. History teaches us that an oppressive system must be counterpoised by a progressive system. As Cabral (1973) observed, "there arose a question of strength, the strength necessary to be pitted against the strength of the colonists."

Scientific Pan-Africanism is the progressive Ideological-system for African people. It seeks four (4) fundamental aims: **1)** establish sovereign status and recognition for the Pan-African community, **2)** abolish and expel all foreign control and neo-colonist domination, operating in Africa, **3)** foster socio-politico solidarity amongst the Pan-African community and **4)** place the destiny of Africa in the hands of authentic Africans, "Only a continental union can save Africa." (Diop, 1986)   Until Africa is a politically and economically self-determining nation, African people everywhere are in jeopardy. On this last point, Dr. Kwame Nkrumah (1973) so eloquently explains:

> Real black freedom will only come when Africa is politically united. It is only then that the black man will be free to breathe the air of freedom, which is his to breathe, in any part of the world. (pp. 14)

Scientific Pan-Africanism advances the position that African people are an ancient people. "We are able to say scientifically today, with certainty, that mankind was born in Africa within the region of Kenya and around the area that comprises Ethiopia and Tanzania..." (Diop, 1986) Africans are the mothers and fathers of civilization; therefore, we cannot be defined by nor limited to national boarders or geographical boundaries. As the mothers and fathers of civilization, African people predate these socio-politico constructs. Scientific Pan-Africanism does not acknowledge any European socio-politico boundaries. Scientific Pan-Africanism holds that African people transcend these boarders and geographical boundaries; thus, we do not recognize the validity of such. We recognize only a worldwide African community, existing throughout the world.

Thus, in the prophetic words of Cheikh Anta Diop (1986):

> A continental African state is a pre-requisite for the survival of black societies wherever they might be. Black communities must find a way to articulate their historical unity. The ties between black Africans and the blacks of Asia, Oceania, the Caribbean, south America and the United States must be strengthened on a rational Basis. (pp. 246)

Therefore, African people living in Africa, Asia, Europe, North America, South America and Australia are Africans. The difference of geographical location does not negate their Africanity: Africa is in their blood, and at the core of their being. Their Africanity cannot be destroyed or purged! Not only are they African but they practice African culture, as well. However, due to different geographical, environmental, political, economic, social and climatic conditions, African culture incorporates different features; thus, taking on many diverse expressions. This does not render them anything other than African culture. Throughout the world, African culture adopts from, reflects and adapts to the many different geo-socio-politico settings.

Cabral (1973) made the following observation concerning culture:

> Whatever may be the ideological or idealistic characteristics of cultural expression, culture is an essential element of the history of a people. ...Culture plunges its roots into the physical reality of the environmental humus in which it develops, and reflects the organic nature of the society, which may be more or less influenced by external factors. (pp. 42)

Scientific Pan-Africanism reject the position of different cultures, distinct and separate, in relation to African people, on the basis that the underlying principles and essence of these, so-called different cultures, are African. Africa is historically and scientifically at the core of each one of these so-called different cultures. Diversity does not negate oneness, nor does it preclude continuity. Therefore, Scientific Pan-Africanism holds that each so-called different African culture is an integral part of an African holistic culture: Pan-African culture. *Pan* signifies, suggest and imply all inclusive and/or all embracing; total, involving everyone. So it follows from this understanding that Scientific Pan-Africanism is concerned with, include and embrace the totality of African people.

Pan speaks to the fact and underscores the reality that African people are a single cultural group, a holistic body politic. Difference in geography does not render African people different people. "We must understand the concept that for us the question of community is not geography, it is a question of us black people, wherever we are." (Toure, 1965) We remain an African people occupying different geographical locations. African people are an extension of one another;

therefore, historically, culturally, politically, socially, economically and spiritually connected.

African people are an organic whole; inextricably tied one to the other. "We are blood of the same blood and flesh of the same flesh." (Toure, 1965) Therefore, the suffering and affliction of an African person anywhere affects African people everywhere.

Kwame Toure (1965) goes on to make the following observation:

> We are Africans. We are scattered all over the Western Hemisphere; black people can be found from south Africa to Nova Scotia. Fifty percent of the population in Brazil: black. In Panama, in Guatemala, in the Dominican Republic, in the West Indies, in the United States, in Canada---we're all over. And we are the same people. (pp. 152)

Scientific Pan-Africanism posits: African people are their greatest resource. African people are a vast reservoir of revolutionary potential. Therefore, the salvation of the Pan-African community and redemption of Africa is the sole responsibility of the Pan-African community. We cannot be naïve and think otherwise; therefore, "we cannot look to our oppressors, those who oppress us, to liberate us or to even help in our liberation. For they will and must serve their own interest, which always involves oppressing us, the African people." (Toure, 1965). This does not mean that African people should refuse genuine help (which is rare). It simply means that African people must be the vanguard of the African liberation Struggle. Scientific

Pan-Africanism is a self-help, self-reliant and self-preservation ideological-system. "The first law of revolution is the law of self-sufficiency."(Toure, 1965)

The total unification and liberation of Africa is a critical strategic aim of the African revolution; a revolution sanctioned in ancestral blood. It is an essential component of the revolutionary storm raging against imperialism, neo-colonialism, classism, sexism, new-age domestic colonialism and racism. "In order to achieve African power, Mother Africa must be strong. To be strong she must be unified." (Toure, 1965) Thus, Scientific Pan-Africanism holds that the realization of a unified and liberated Africa is hinged upon the destruction of the imperialism and neo-colonialism in Africa. "As long as a single foot of African soil remains under foreign domination, the battle must continue." (Nkrumah, 1963)

Dr. Kwame Nkrumah (1963) in his informative book Africa Must Unite had the following to say concerning African unity:

> Problems resulting from the cynical parceling-out of Africa still remain, and can only be settled by continental union. (pp. 7)

Dr. Nkrumah continues:

> The unity of the countries of Africa is an indispensable precondition for The speediest and fullest development, not only of the totality of the Continent but of the individual countries linked together in the union. (pp. 163, 164)

He further elaborates:

> We are Africans first and last, and as Africans
> our best interests can only Be served by uniting
> within an African community. (pp. 217)

African unity is inextricably tied to African liberation. Therefore, disunity precludes African liberation. The humanity of Africa depends upon the unification of African people. This must be the millennium of African ascension, and the consolidation of Pan-African solidarity. For Pan-African solidarity is the key to Pan-African Empowerment! *"Today, the only viable political solution for Africa is in a continental state."* (Diop, 1986) The survival of African people rests upon the psychosocial, political and economic unity of Africa. African unity is crucial because, "...the fact remains that a continental federation is an urgently vital necessity for the totality of African peoples...it is the pre-condition for our collective survival. (Diop, 1986)

The redemption of Africa is at the heart of Scientific Pan-Africanism. Africa is a central and prominent theme permeating Scientific Pan African thought and practice. Which is largely about regrouping, reconnecting and reconstructing; thus, reconstituting an operational whole of African people, to facilitate the realization of African unity and liberation. This is indispensable to Scientific Pan-African thought and practice. African solidarity, with great emphasis on collective identity, collective personality and collective consciousness, is an underlying dynamic of Scientific Pan-Africanism. Our success and failure as a people is inextricably tied together; African people are interrelated. Therefore, "The future of blacks all over the world is interconnected. It was so in the past when black civilizations were under serious pressure. It is even more so at present..." (Diop, 1986)

Scientific Pan-Africanism holds that African people are an organic whole, sharing a common destiny. It further advances the position that African people are an extension of one another. Nevertheless, African people are confronted with the challenge of self-perception. African people must cultivate a healthy perception of self. For the manner in which you respond to a thing is often times dictated by how the thing is perceived. Therefore, the manner in which African people respond and relate to one another is dictated by African people's perception of one another. Moreover, the manner in which we relate to the world is also dictated by our perception of one another. Worldview is greatly influenced by self-perception, and self-perception is shaped by culture. This would explain the distorted perception that African people have of one another. Having endured the Maafa on the continent and in the Diaspora, African people have suffered a cultural assault leaving them culturally displaced. Thus, cultural displacement dis-figured and distorted our self-perception.

Section eight
Systematic Oppression

New-Age Domestic Colonialism

New-age Domestic Colonialism is colonialism by mutual agreement. It is a symbiotic relationship whereby one group accepts the status of colonial subjects. This is the logical consequence of being a victim of Neo-oppression! Neo-oppression is a psycho-technological oppression, post-modern oppression, but oppression nonetheless. The unique thing of which is: 1) it's sophisticated, 2) it's subtle and 3) it's self-imposed. Therefore, it must be understood as a systematic perpetuation of oppression whereby the oppressed unwittingly assume responsibility for maintaining and sustaining their own state of oppression. Thus, Neo-oppression facilitates and consolidates the repressive and debilitating socio-economic system of New-age Domestic Colonialism.

This is a high-tech yet insidious form of colonialism established and implemented within the national boarders of the U. S. A. Consistent with all forms of colonialism, New-age Domestic Colonialism serves a pure politico-economic agenda: the monopolization and concentration of capital in the hands of a minority ruling class, and the appropriation of labor power. It is about the exploitation of human resources to enrich and advance industrial-corporate merchants. The talents, skills, technical genius and intellectual prowess, of African people, are exploited, in an attempt, to satisfy an insatiable appetite of a small clique of industrial-corporate merchants. This parasitic ruling class capitalize off the labor power, abilities and mental faculties of subjugated African communities; thereby, empowering itself.

The exploitation of African people, within the U. S. A., is executed in such a subtle and inconspicuous manner that the majority of African people do not realize it. Therefore, they accept and ultimately partake in their own exploitation. This is largely due to ignorance and mis-education. Integrating into and becoming a part of the socio-economic system responsible for the oppression and exploitation of African people can only serve to re-enforce the existence of oppression and exploitation. The failure to challenge and check this twin evil strengthens and consolidates it. Thus, its very existence is predicated upon the existence of a subjugated and nonresistant African community.

Our eagerness and willingness to be a part of this system makes possible our collective oppression. This is the foundation of New-age Domestic Colonialism. The system is built on and situates itself upon the service African people renders to the socio-economic arrangement within the U. S. A. Accepting and acting out on the belief that we can benefit individually perpetuates our collective oppression. On this point Dr. Wilson is clear "The power of whites as a group to dominate and exploit Blacks as a group is primarily due to their manipulative inculcation in Blacks of the belief in the mythology of individualism..." (1998)

New-age Domestic Colonialism, as it has emerged and developed within the U. S. A., is the existence of an un-equal and unjust, forced relation, between Euro-Americans and Africans. This strange state of relation is described as follows: a socio-economic relationship of oppression, exploitation and repression premised on the domination of the former and the subjugation of the latter. Europeans exercise politico and economic power, and they are the designers of social policies. On this last point, Dr. Wilson (1998) made the following observation:

> ...powerful groups derive their ability to establish the "rules of the game" from their having achieved by some preliminary means (not necessarily legitimate) the important resources which enables them to impose their self-serving rules on others in the first place. (pp. 167)

African communities, within the U. S. A., live a precarious and powerless existence. We control neither the politics nor the economics affecting and influencing our lives; control is in the hands of industrial-corporate merchants. This type of relationship is debilitating by nature. It obstructs, restricts and thwarts the productive development of the African community, while exploiting the labor-power and resources therein; thus, fostering the productive development of Euro-Americans. This is the basis of a colonial relationship: the socio-economic construction of a situation wherein one cultural group is constrained and compelled to labor in the service of another cultural group, to empower said cultural group, while simultaneously depriving itself of power.

Manning Marable (1983), in his highly informative and instructive book How Capitalism Underdeveloped Black America made the following analysis:

> Slavery and colonialism created the material conditions which forced an oppressed people to leave the surroundings of their previous history. That is, the external constraints demanded by coerced labor and a rigid caste/social hierarchy redirect the forces of a people's history. The slave could not live for him/herself at any particular moment during the productive process; the slave was viewed by the master as a cog in the accumulation of capital. (pp. 26)

Therefore, African communities are dependent upon and subordinate to the dominant industrial-corporate economy. The economic existence of African people is at the whims of a group of merchants. This minority class ultimately controls all regulatory factors (management of production, distribution, consumption etc.). Let me put it another way, the African community is under the sway of a profit driven extraneous inimical gentry: New-age Merchants. They have managed to contrive an economic situation that incapacitates and subsequently under-develops African communities; thereby, rendering our communities weak, vulnerable, dependent and exploitable. Thus, the economic existence of African people serves to buttress and build up the industrial-corporate economy, at the expense of African people. The service and labor provided by African people, within the U. S. A., does not secure, preserve and perpetuate the welfare of African people. Neither is our finances expended in promoting and advancing the socio-politico-economic well-being of African people.

A small clique of merchants manipulates the collective buying power of African people, within the U. S. A., for the sole purpose of bolstering up their political and economic power to consolidate their interest. The realization of which requires taking advantage of Afrikan people: mis-used, abused, under-paid and systematically deprived of employ-ment. This type of socio-economic arrangement constrains African people to live at a subsistence level (just getting by, from paycheck to paycheck). To subsist is vulnerability and weakness! No production or progress can come from such a socio-economic arrangement. It can only contribute to the existing power, dominance and control of Euro-Americans over African people. This is an un-healthy state of affairs. Therefore, it weighs heavy upon us, as a cultural group, to rectify the current socio-economic arrangement. African people must not continue submitting to the power-powerless relationship that exists between Europeans and us.

We are charged with the task of learning how not to just subsist (slaves subsist). A subsistence existence is static and immobile! No good come to a people who just subsist. For it is inconsistent with self-determination. A self-determining people are a vibrant, developing, progressing and evolving people. They are a people who dictate the terms of their own existence. Therefore, African people must start focusing on their own socio-politico and economic empowerment, to become a cultural force. Nevertheless, how can this come to realization when we are: **1)** caught up in the vicious cycle of living from paycheck to paycheck, **2)** trapped in the pernicious system of debt bondage, and **3)** slaves to the debilitating habit of conspicuous consumption? These behavior habits and life styles hinders and stifles our productive development; thus, preventing our political and economic rise to independence. In short, these habits are slavish; thus, rendering African people victims of Euro-American slavery: New-age Domestic Colonialism.

As long as the politics and economics, of African communities, are controlled and dictated externally, by an extraneous force, then the economy therein will remain pitifully dependent upon and subordinate to the industrial-corporate economy of Euro-America. This type of economic aggression is indispensable to the existence and perpetuation of the monstrous system of New-age Domestic Colonialism. The current politico-economic status of Africans, within the U. S. A., is essential to and ensures the political and economic dominance and control of Euro-America; thus, their power rest upon our powerlessness. The situation can best be described and expressed as such: figuratively, Euro-America is the superstructure of a magnificent edifice and the talents, skills, intellectual prowess, technical genius and labor power of African people is the foundation upon which this impressive structure rest.

Thus, the subservient and subordinate socio-economic-politico position of the African community is due to our inability to organize around our common interest, deduced from a realistic assessment of our existing socio-economic-politico conditions. We cannot be afraid to admit the truth as it pertains to the redemption of African people. Healing of any kind involves honesty. By extension, in order to administer to an ailment or disease of any kind you must first make an accurate diagnosis of the ailment or disease in order to make a proper prognosis to effect healing. Therefore, the socio-politico- economic disease from which African people (in the U.S.A) suffer is New-age Domestic Colonialism: Slavery.

New-age Domestic Colonialism is a 21st century mode of slavery, which seeks the same objective as every other mode of slavery: to dominate, control, subjugate and dictate the socio-politico-economic existence of another cultural group. Thus, as all modes of slavery are, New-age Domestic Colonialism is repressive and exploitative, which, by its very nature, spawns the socio-economic condition of poverty. This renders poverty an artificially manufactured thing within human society. The logic behind this reasoning is simple; if New-age Domestic Colonialism, which is a Euro-American manufactured repressive economic system, spawns poverty then logically poverty, as it relate to African people, is a Euro-American manufactured phenomenon. There is nothing natural about poverty, and just because it is common amongst African people does not mean it is natural.

Poverty dampens spirits, kills aspirations, breeds dismay and gives rise to despair, which in turn gives birth to low self-esteem, lack of self-respect and a negative self-image. This is the social matrix wherein apathy, anomy and criminality are born. These degenerative behavior characteristics threaten the economic empowerment and socio-politico advancement of the African community. Consistent with the social dynamics of society, an apathetic and anomic people are a selfish, reckless and individualistic people. Thus, they are a people politically naïve and socially un-conscious; thus, prone to crime. By extension, this type of people is mentally disoriented, psychologically subjugated and historically anemic. All of which are essential to the perpetuation of New-age Domestic Colonialism.

Fundamental to the existence of New-age Domestic Colonialism is a people whose consciousness has been subverted and inverted to the point that it is easy to put them at odds with one another; thereby, fragmenting them as a people. This ultimately breeds intra-group distrust, which precludes unity. Thus, a disunited people are unwitting allies of their enemy. Their dis-united state of existence facilitates the solidification, consolidation and perpetuation of their slavish existence. New-age Domestic Colonialism feeds off and thrives on dis-unity. This type of slavery requires the participation of African people in order for it to be effective. Our cooperation is necessary. It becomes imperative to fracture our consciousness and deprive us of self-knowledge.

New-age Domestic Colonialism deteriorates intra-group relations. This in turn engenders an atmosphere of intra-group disruption and corruption. Thus, eroding the moral fiber therein, contaminating the existing social structure, giving birth to social impurities such as dishonesty, deception, treachery, dishonor, envy, competition and self-hatred. These severely interfere with and interrupt the process of coming together and working together. This, subsequently, makes unity impossible, which strengthens the unification of Euro-America. The destruction of African unity is conducive to the maintenance and sustenance of New-age Domestic Colonialism. A disunited and distrustful people are everywhere and always a doomed people! As long as African people remain disunited and choose not to acknowledge the reality of their socio-politico and economic situation, their subjugated and slavish state will remain a fact of their existence. Slavery is in effect!

The African community in the 21st century is contending with slavery in the mode of New-age Domestic Colonialism, which is a power-dynamic relationship: White power and African American powerlessness. On this matter, Dr. Wilson (1998) had the following to say:

> The power relationship between Blacks and Whites is an interactive one—one where White power, to a significant extent, arises out of certain types of social Interactions between Whites and Blacks where Blacks unwittingly play a very Important role in constituting and sustaining their powerlessness relative to Whites. (pp. 357)

New-age Domestic Colonialism eviscerates and devours African communities. Moreover, New-age Domestic Colonialism arrests the development of and subsequently under-develop African communities to the point that a process of retrogression is set in motion. The African community takes a retrograde step backwards. Prosperity and progress is obstructed and halted! At this point adverse and backward motion commences. The entire socio-economic system is erosive and debilitating to the core. African communities must be economically strangled, politically stunted and socially malnourished in order for New-age Domestic Colonialism to fuel itself and persist. This is made possible with the aid of infected Africans, that is, African people who think like Europeans. Africans with European mentalities will always serve the interest of Europeans at the expense of African people. To paraphrase Malcolm X: be not deceived by those who look like you but think like the oppressor. The so-called African American elite! They often time sympathize with the system of oppression because they benefit from it, at the expense of the majority of African people. This is what Manning Marable (1983) wrote concerning that issue:

> The elite was a privileged social stratum...who praised the master publicly if not Privately; who fashioned its religious rituals, educational norms, and social Structures on those of the west; who sought to accumulate petty amounts of Capital at the expense of their Black sisters and brothers. (pp. 24)

Largely, there are many African people, within the U. S. A., who are complicit in maintaining New-age Domestic Colonialism. Due to ignorance, mental disorientation and psychological subjugation many of us conduct ourselves in a manner, although seemingly beneficial, is not beneficial to our collective empowerment. Our actions serve the material and financial interest of our oppressor. We have been deluded into believing that the acquisition and accumulation of exorbitant sums of capital will somehow solve our socio-politico-economic situation. Thus, in a frenzy, we begin chasing the illusion of getting rich, attempting to amass all the finances that we can (in hopes of becoming wealthy). In the midst of it all, we lose ourselves and become slaves of things: addicts of material possessions. During this process moral and ethical principles are abandoned, values are disregarded, spirituality sacrificed and integrity compromised. Subsequently greed, cynicism and selfishness are born.

New-age Domestic Colonialism conditions within African people the survival-of-the-fittest mentality, the attitude of everyone for him or herself, detached and dislocated individualism. Crude individualism is a contradiction in nature. Dr. Wilson (1998) had the following to say concerning this individualism:

> The ideological pablum of individualism fed to Black America produces in that community the concept of the individual as one who "exists as something abstracted from a social matrix, apart from the web of tasks, obligations, affections, and collective relationships which give people their identities, their social meaning, and their experience of humanity and of themselves. (pp. 150)

This type of mindset is counter-productive to the socio-economic empowerment of African people. Operating with this mentality engenders and re-enforces intra-group distrust and fosters division within our communities. When this occurs, it blinds us to the reality that we share the same fate; thus, inextricably bound up in the same plight. African people are tied one to the other socially, economically, politically and culturally. As long as we remain ignorant to this reality, our actions will continue to run counter to our collective interest. Thus, we will continue being the oil fueling the evil machinery of New-age Domestic Colonialism.

As long as African people continue thinking in terms of me, myself and I, we will never usher in the type of radical and progressive change needed to break the psychosocial restraints that binds us. We will never improve upon our social, political and economic conditions if we remain a fragmented and disunited people. This serves the economic interest of the industrial-corporate merchant class. Our internal weaknesses bolster up a parasitic economic system that feeds on and live off the appropriation of our labor power and the exploitation of our skills and talents. Thus, "The motor of modern capitalist world accumulation was driven by the labor power of Afro-American slaves." (Marable, 1983) This mode of operation persists! The political aim of this vampire system is to consign and relegate African communities to an inferior socio-economic position in hopes of rendering African communities permanent UrBan Colonies.

Our politico-economic condition is a colonial situation. However, we have yet to realize it. This is due largely to the fact that we assess and analyze our situation from an individualistic position: we erroneously believe that individual financial gain is collective progress. This can be the furthest from the truth. For instance, during the times of chattel slavery there were some Africans who had acquired finances and owned business, yet slavery remained a fact for African people. The existence of African woman and men who had accumulated finances and established businesses did not change the fact that: **1)** African people were politically dominated, **2)** African people were socially controlled and **3)** African people were economically exploited. This holds true for African people today. Just because some of us have accumulated substantial amounts of finances and own businesses does not mean that African people are not subjected to an internal domestic colonial situation.

New-age Domestic Colonialism is colonialism; however, it differs slightly in expression and execution from the traditional form of colonialism and neo-colonialism. For instance, colonialism (among other things) is a socio-politico-economic system whereby a foreign nation invades, socially control, politically dominate and economically exploits another nation: repress the indigenous people and appropriate their labor power and natural resources. By extension, political and economic power is exercised from the mother country; thus, rendering the indigenous people dependent subjects of a foreign nation. This is typical of traditional colonialism.

On the other hand, Neo-colonialism is an extension and consequence of colonialism in that it is a politically modified version, wherein Political authority is conceded to the indigenous people; however, the colonial empire retains economic power. Neo-colonialism can be described as follows: political figureheads are picked from amongst the indigenous people, and placed in administrative positions. This is nominal independence at best: independence in appearance only, devoid of real political and economic power to concretize and secure said independence. Moreover, under a Neo-colonial regime the previous economic situation persist: cheap labor, appropriation of labor power, selfish exploitation of natural resources, repression, etc. The only thing that is truly different is the perpetrator is of the indigenous people. In essence, the colonial empire dictates the political and economic destiny of the Neo-colonial regime.

Dr. Kwame Nkrumah (1965) describes it best:

> The essence of neo-colonialism is that the state which is subject to it is, in theory, independent and has all the outward trappings of international sovereignty. In reality its economic system and thus its political policy is directed from outside. (pp. ix)

Indispensable to the security and perpetuation of New-age Domestic Colonialism is a standing domestic police force, Gestapo style, policing African communities, enforcing a colonial brand of law and order: organized repression. The primary function of this police force is to: **1)** terrorize, **2)** execute sham arrests, **3)** harass, **4)** contain and **5)** pretend to serve the people. Its entire existence is a pretense; it does not serve the people. If it did, African people would not be stereotyped, stigmatized or viewed with unwarranted suspicion by the police force. The police force (city, state and federal) exists to serve and protect the interest of a specific class of people: industrial-corporate merchants. This explains why it functions, in relation to the African community, like an occupying force. Thus, the police serve as an instrument of repression and containment to keep the African community in check, subservient, intimidated and subjugated. By doing so, forcing African people to comply with and conform to the rules of industrial-corporate merchants.

A logical extension of the standing police force is a sophisticated industrial prison complex, with a burgeoning private sector. This is an integral part and essential function of New-age Domestic Colonialism. The industrial prison complex serves as a legal instrument of repression against political and revolutionary dissenters, and it warehouses an exploitable labor force. Prison provides a source of cheap labor! Those with a stake in the industrial prison complex appropriate the labor power of prisoners. The industrial prison complex is a *neo-plantation* via, the 13th Amendment to the United States Constitution (1865), and I quote:

> Neither slavery nor involuntary servitude, except as a punishment for Crime whereof the party shall have been duly convicted, shall exist Within the United States, or any place subject to their jurisdiction

Clearly this amendment is saying that slavery can exist within the jurisdiction of the United States when "the party shall have been duly convicted". This means that once someone is convicted she or he can be and will be subjected to the status of a slave. The question becomes: how is the convictions brought about? Poverty is systematically manufactured to induce desperation within the impoverished. Thus, in a desperate attempt to escape an impoverished situation (to acquire finances) crime is committed. This, undoubtedly, leads to arrests, convictions and ultimately subjection to slave like conditions on a *neo-plantation*---the industrial prison complex. Therefore, it must be understood that the entire penal system is a socio-politico instrument instituted to serve an economic interest.

Most UrBan crime is economically motivated. Economic factors induce and influence UrBan crime in many ways. Unfavorable and imbalanced economic conditions, which are manufactured, breed and spur crime! Criminality is transgressive behavior born (in most cases) of a poverty-stricken environment. Considering the fact poverty is an artificially manufactured condition, we logically infer that the UrBan criminal is an artificially manufactured social product. The Urban criminal is necessary to the existence of the capitalist mode of production, which expresses itself in and through New-age Domestic Colonialism. The UrBan criminal serves as a pretext to disguise the true politico-economic function of the police force, which is to protect the material interest of the industrial corporate merchants. Thus, the *so-called* war on crime is a war against the downtrodden: disadvantaged, dispossessed, displaced, disenfranchised, dis-educated and disdained.

The police force exists to ensure the well-being of the industrial-corporate merchant class. The police are the guardians of the industrial-corporate merchant's law, which is the embodiment of their will. Therefore, it must be understood that the police force (city, state and federal) functions to protect the property, interest and privileges of the industrial-corporate merchant class, and their vampire dog-eat-dog economic arrangement: capitalism. Thus, the police force is a security force, for the haves against the have-nots, necessary to ensuring the existence of industrial-corporate rule: Euro-American hegemony.

New-age Domestic Colonialism is a parasitic socio-politico-economic system by nature. Thus, in order for it to survive, grow and thrive it must feed off the exploitation of resources (natural and human). New-age Domestic Colonialism is a violent and criminal economic excrescence of the capitalist mode of production. The nature of which is selfishness and greed. Capitalism, and all of its subsystems, follows the dictates of an unwritten capitalist law: acquire, amass and monopolize all the capital that you can, and subjugate, oppress, exploit and colonize whomever in the process.

Section nine
Closing

For all too long Europeans have taken it upon themselves to conceptualize and define for African people. These concepts and definitions are imposed upon African people and presented as universal. As a result of this, African people have made the dreadful mistake of accepting these concepts and definitions without question or analysis; without African-centered scrutiny. Even some of our brightest minds have committed this sin: the sin of intellectual laxness. We must never relax our intellectual vigilance in the face of protracted cultural aggression. This is all we have received from Europeans since our first encounter.

The time is long overdue for this vicious habit to cease; we can no longer commit the sin of intellectual laxness. African people must stop accepting, as valid and universal, European concepts and definitions and start questioning and analyzing European concepts and definitions (from an African perspective). European history doesn't give African people any reason not to examine their concepts and definitions. Europeans do not have exclusive authority to conceptualize and define; therefore, their concepts and definition are not absolute. In fact, their concepts and definitions are culturally determined (as all concepts and definitions are). This is reason enough to examine their concepts and definitions.

I hope UrBan Philosophy ignite within African people a fire to take on the task of conceptualizing and defining anew. African people must develop their own concepts and define their own reality. For all that lies before our eyes are realized concepts. Europeans have taken it upon themselves to define reality for everyone, by universalizing their concepts and definitions. Acceptance of these concepts and definitions without scrutiny is an act of submission to the dictates of European reality. Concepts define reality. In fact, concepts shape and mold perception to conform to reality. Thus, European concepts shape the perception of African people to conform to European reality. This is a reality that does not promote the wellbeing of African people. Therefore, African people are justified in their rejection of European reality.

Reality is always defined in the best interest of the definer. This means European reality is defined in the best interest of Europeans. Their reality is defined from their point of view, for their benefit. African people don't fit into their socio-politico-economic design (at least not as beneficiaries). Unless African people start defining their own reality, from an African-centered perspective, in their own interest, they will remain a perpetual victim of European reality. There is no time to waste, African people must conceptualize and define for themselves. The time is now!

Afterword

UrBan Philosophy, the concept, entered my mind in the year 1997. It began as Street Philosophy. This is how I initially conceived of it. It wasn't until the year 2000, while incarcerated at the Maryland Correctional Training Center (MCTC), located in Hagerstown Maryland, that I changed it to UrBan Philosophy. I was serving a 20 year sentence for armed robbery (of which I served 13 years and 9 months). Sadly, this time period of incarceration is where I acquired my education. It's not what many would call formal education (if such a thing exist), but it's education nonetheless. In fact, it's the epitome of education: self-knowledge.

Self-knowledge is the path that I eventually embarked upon while incarcerated, which is the path that I continue to tread today (10 years after being released from prison, in 2004). Self-knowledge is the basis of true education! While incarcerated I was able to cultivate a proper understanding of African History and develop an appreciation for African culture. The more I studied and reflected upon African History and African culture, the better I understood the world. My perspective of life began to change; my social awareness increased and my political consciousness broadened. As I continued to study my thinking underwent a metamorphosis, which was the beginning of UrBan Philosophical thought.

UrBan Philosophy emerged as a corrective measure to the mediocrity of thought pervasive within society. As I reflected upon the different levels of thought processes that I encountered, among Africa people, I realized African people were mis-educated and suffered from an acute case of mentacide. Their minds were corrupted by this European reality! As I continued to converse with and engage African people intellectually, the clearer I became about a need for an intellectual overhaul for African people. There was a need for a new way of thinking; thus, a new way of conceiving, perceiving, defining and interfacing with reality.

Mediocrity was the norm that I too often encountered. This didn't set well with my spirit because my study of African History and Culture had informed me of the intellectual and spiritual capacity of African people. I was clearly aware of the genius of African people; they were intellectual giants and spiritual masters. African people were supreme architects and superb engineers. They were healers of the soul, and cultivators of cosmic consciousness. Therefore, it was no way that I could sit by and not put forth an honest effort to add to the greatness of African people; to redeem African people. So, I began to engage in serious contemplation about the African way, which led to a deeper understanding of African Deep Thought. This enabled me to arrive at the conclusion: the African way is an orderly and harmonious way; highly structured and governed by high morals and sound principles. It is a life-centered way; a pro-nature way. It is a way that promotes growth and development and it cultivates the highest essence of the African man and woman. Thus, the African way fosters the evolution of the African mind; thereby, facilitating human perfectibility.

Knowing this is what African people once were gave rise to UrBan Philosophy. I began to reflect upon and organize my thoughts into a progressive system consistent with the African way. Therefore, UrBan Philosophy emerges as a continuation of the great works of African people. As a thought and behavior system, UrBan Philosophy seeks to enhance the thinking and performance of African people; to master excellence. The idea is to encourage African people to change their thinking and behaving; to enhance the way they interface with reality, to challenge African people to be themselves. We are our ancestors; therefore, we must be as our ancestors were.

UrBan Philosophy is a mental enema, intellectual laxative and a cultural detoxification for African people. African people have to be purged of European ways of thinking and being. Therefore, African people must regain their ability to think and behave on a higher level; to think and behave as their ancestors.

Writing this book has been a wonderful experience for me. I enjoyed the entire process and I hope you enjoyed the read. Look forward to my next book: Politics of UrBan Struggle. Coming soon!

Imhotep Asis Fatiu

Suggested Reading

1. From The Browder File: Anthony T. Browder
2. Nile Valley Contribution To Civilization: Anthony T. Browder
3. Afrocentricity: Dr. Molefi K. Asante
4. Stolen Legacy: George G. M. James
5. African People In world History: John H. Clarke
6. African Glory: J. C. deGraft-Johnson
7. Introduction To African Civilization: John G. Jackson
8. The Destruction of Black Civilization: Chancellor Williams
9. The Falsification of Afrikan Consciousness: Amos Wilson
10. Cultural Misorientation: Dr. Kobi K. K. Kambon
11. The African Personality In America: Dr. K. K. Kambon
12. African Power: Asa Hilliard
13. Let The Circle Be Unbroken: Marimba Ani
14. The Book of The Coming forth By Day: Dr. Maulana Karenga
15. The Husia: Dr. Maulana Karenga
16. Essays In Ancient Egyptian Studies: Jacob Carruthers
17. African Psychology: Dr. Wade Nobles
18. Africana Womanism: Clenora Hudson-Weems
19. Post Traumatic Slave Syndrome: Dr. Joy DeGruy Leary
20. Return To The African Mother Principle of Male and Female Equality: Dr. Oba T'shaka0
21. Centered: Mwalimu Baruti
22. Mentacide: Mwalimu Baruti

References

Abdul-Raheem, T. (1996). *Pan Africanism: politics, economy and social change in the Twenty-first century.* New York, NY: New York Press.

Cabral, A. (1973). Return To The Source: Selected speeches of Amilcar Cabral New York, NY: Monthly Review Press.

Diop, A. C. (1986). *Great African Thinkers.* New Brunswick, NJ: Transaction Books.

Esedebe, O. P. (1980). *Pan-Africanism: the idea and movement, 1176-1991.* Washington, DC: Howard University Press.

Hilliard, G. A. (1997). *SBA: the reawakening of the African mind.* Gainesville, FL: Makare Publishing Company.

Marable, M. (1983). *How Capitalism Underdeveloped Black America.* Cambridge, MA: South end Press

Nkrumah, K. (1973). *The Struggle Continues.* London, UK: Panaf Books.

Nrumah, K. (1965). *Neo-Colonialism: the last stage of imperialism.* New York, NY: International Publishes

Nkrumah, K. (1963). *Africa Must Unite.* London, UK: Panaf Books.

Padmore, G. (1956). *Pan-Africanism or Communism: the coming struggle for Africa* London, UK: Dennis Dobson

Ture, K. (1965). *Stokely Speaks: from black power to pan-Africanism* Chicago, IL: Chicago Review Press

Wilson, A. (1998). Blueprint for Black power: *a moral, political and economic imperative for the twenty-first century.* Brooklyn, NY: Afrikan World Infosystems